LIBERTY

AND

TYRANNY

A CONSERVATIVE MANIFESTO

Mark R. Levin

THRESHOLD EDITIONS

NEW YORK   LONDON   TORONTO   SYDNEY

Threshold Editions
A Division of Simon & Schuster, Inc.
1230 Avenue of the Americas
New York, NY 10020

First Threshold Editions hardcover edition March 2009

THRESHOLD EDITIONS and colophon are trademarks of Simon & Schuster, Inc.

For information about special discounts for bulk purchases,
please contact Simon & Schuster Special Sales at
1-866-506-1949 or business@simonandschuster.com.

The Simon & Schuster Speakers Bureau can bring authors to your live event.
For more information or to book an event contact the Simon & Schuster Speakers
Bureau at 866-248-3049 or visit our website at www.simonspeakers.com.

Designed by Joy O'Meara

Manufactured in the United States of America

7   9   10   8

ISBN-13: 978-1-4165-6285-6
ISBN-10:   1-4165-6285-0

To my family and fellow countrymen

ACKNOWLEDGMENTS

A SPECIAL THANK-YOU TO my family for their love, support, and forbearance throughout this long process, and who have always encouraged me in everything I do.

I want to thank Eric Christensen for his many invaluable contributions throughout this project, and David Limbaugh for his good judgment and wise counsel. Thanks also to my colleagues at Landmark Legal Foundation Richard Hutchison, Michael O'Neill, and Matthew Forys for their excellent insights and research assistance. My editor, Mitchell Ivers of Simon & Schuster, always makes my books better. And to my friends Rush Limbaugh, Sean Hannity, Ed Meese, and Mary Matalin for their constant inspiration and support.

I also want to acknowledge the champions of liberty—the great philosophers, scholars, visionaries, and statesmen—on whose shoulders we all stand; the hero warriors who gave birth to America and continue to protect her; and the American people, who have contributed so much to mankind.

CONTENTS

1

ON LIBERTY AND TYRANNY

THERE IS SIMPLY NO scientific or mathematical formula that defines conservatism. Moreover, there are competing voices today claiming the mantle of "true conservatism"—including neo-conservatism (emphasis on a robust national security), paleo-conservatism (emphasis on preserving the culture), social conservatism (emphasis on faith and values), and libertarianism (emphasis on individualism), among others. Scores of scholars have written at length about what can be imperfectly characterized as conservative thought. But my purpose is not to give them each exposition, as it cannot be fairly or adequately accomplished here, nor referee among them. Neither will I attempt to give birth to totally new theories.

Instead, what follows are my own opinions and conclusions of fundamental truths, based on decades of observation, exploration, and experience, about conservatism and, conversely, non-conservatism—that is, liberty and tyranny in modern America.

To put it succinctly: Conservatism is a way of understanding life, society, and governance. The Founders were heavily influenced by certain philosophers, among them Adam Smith (spontaneous order), Charles Montesquieu (separation of powers), and especially John Locke (natural rights); they were also influenced by their faiths, personal experiences, and knowledge of history (including the rise and fall of the Roman Empire). Edmund Burke, who was both a British statesman and thinker, is often said to be the father of modern conservatism. He was an early defender of the American Revolution and advocate of representative government. He wrote of the interconnection of liberty, free markets, religion, tradition, and authority. The Conservative, like the Founders, is informed by all these great thinkers—and more.

The Declaration of Independence represents the most prominent, official, consensus position of the Founders' rationale for declaring independence from England. It states, in part,

> *When in the Course of human events it becomes necessary for one people to dissolve the political bands which have connected them with another and to assume among the powers of the earth, the separate and equal station to which* the Laws of Nature and of Nature's God *entitle them, a decent respect to the opinions of mankind requires that they should declare the causes which impel them to the separation.* We hold these truths to be self-evident, that all men are created equal, that they are endowed by their Creator with certain unalienable Rights, that among these are Life, Liberty and the pursuit of Happiness. . . .

The Founders believed, and the Conservative agrees, in the dignity of the individual; that we, as human beings, have a right to live, live freely, and pursue that which motivates us not because man or some government says so, but because these are God-given natural rights.

Like the Founders, the Conservative also recognizes in society a *harmony of interests*,[1] as Adam Smith put it, and rules of cooperation that have developed through generations of human experience and collective reasoning that promote the betterment of the individual and society. This is characterized as ordered liberty, the social contract, or *the civil society*.

What are the conditions of this civil society?

In the civil society, the *individual* is recognized and accepted as more than an abstract statistic or faceless member of some group; rather, he is a *unique, spiritual being* with a soul and a conscience. He is free to discover his own potential and pursue his own legitimate interests, tempered, however, by a *moral order* that has its foundation in *faith* and guides his life and all human life through the *prudent* exercise of judgment. As such, the individual in the civil society strives, albeit imperfectly, to be virtuous—that is, restrained, ethical, and honorable. He rejects the relativism that blurs the lines between good and bad, right and wrong, just and unjust, and means and ends.

In the civil society, the individual has a *duty* to respect the unalienable rights of others and the values, customs, and traditions, tried and tested over time and passed from one generation to the next, that establish society's *cultural identity*. He is responsible for attending to his own well-being and that of his family. And he has a duty as a *citizen* to contribute voluntarily to the welfare of his community through good works.

In the civil society, *private property* and liberty are inseparable. The individual's right to live freely and safely and pursue happiness includes the right to acquire and possess property, which represents the fruits of his own intellectual and/or physical labor. As the individual's time on earth is finite, so, too, is his labor. The illegitimate denial or diminution of his private property enslaves him to another and denies him his liberty.

In the civil society, a *rule of law*, which is just, known, and predictable, and applied equally albeit imperfectly, provides the governing framework for and restraints on the polity, thereby nurturing the civil society and serving as a check against the arbitrary use and, hence, abuse of power.[2]

For the Conservative, the civil society has as its highest purpose its preservation and improvement.[3]

The Modern Liberal believes in the supremacy of the state, thereby rejecting the principles of the Declaration and the order of the civil society, in whole or part. For the Modern Liberal, the individual's imperfection and personal pursuits impede the objective of a utopian state. In this, Modern Liberalism promotes what French historian Alexis de Tocqueville described as a *soft tyranny*,[4] which becomes increasingly more oppressive, potentially leading to a hard tyranny (some form of totalitarianism). As the word *"liberal"* is, in its classical meaning, the opposite of authoritarian, it is more accurate, therefore, to characterize the Modern Liberal as a *Statist*.

The Founders understood that the greatest threat to liberty is an all-powerful central government, where the few dictate to the many. They also knew that the rule of the mob would lead to anarchy and, in the end, despotism. During the Revolutionary War, the states more or less followed the Articles of Confederation, in which most governing authority remained with the states.

After the war, as the Founders labored to establish a new nation, the defects with the Articles became increasingly apparent. The central government did not have the ability to fund itself. Moreover, states were issuing their own currency, conducting their own foreign policy, and raising their own armies. Trade disputes among the states and with other countries were hampering commerce and threatening national prosperity.

Eventually the Articles were replaced with the Constitution, which granted the federal government enough authority to cultivate, promote, and "secure the Blessings of Liberty to ourselves and our Posterity,"[5] but not enough authority to destroy it all. James Madison, the most influential of the Constitution's authors, put it best when he wrote in "Federalist 51":

> But what is government itself, but the greatest of all reflections on human nature? If men were angels, no government would be necessary. If angels were to govern men, neither external nor internal controls on government would be necessary. In framing a government which is to be administered by men over men, the great difficulty lies in this: you must first enable the government to control the governed; and in the next place oblige it to control itself.[6]

For much of American history, the balance between governmental authority and individual liberty was understood and accepted. Federal power was confined to that which was specifically enumerated in the Constitution and no more. And that power was further limited, for it was dispersed among three federal branches—the legislative, executive, and judicial. Beyond that, the power remained with the states and ultimately the people.

The Framers recognized that the Constitution may require adjustments from time to time. Therefore, they provided two methods for proposing amendments, only one of which has been used in adopting all current amendments. It requires a supermajority of two-thirds of the members of both Houses of Congress to propose an amendment to the states for ratification, and three-fourths of the states to successfully ratify the proposed amendment. In all our history the Constitution has been amended only twenty-seven times—the first ten of which, the Bill of Rights, were adopted shortly after the Constitution was ratified. Clearly the Framers did not intend the Constitution to be easily altered. It was to be a lasting contract that could be modified only by the considered judgment of a significant representation of the body politic.

But in the 1930s, during the Great Depression, the Statists successfully launched a counterrevolution that radically and fundamentally altered the nature of American society. President Franklin Roosevelt and an overwhelmingly Democratic Congress, through an array of federal projects, entitlements, taxes, and regulations known as the New Deal, breached the Constitution's firewalls. At first the Supreme Court fought back, striking down New Deal programs as exceeding the limits of federal constitutional authority, violating state sovereignty, and trampling on private property rights. But rather than seek an expansion of federal power through the amendment process, which would likely have blunted Roosevelt's ambitions, Roosevelt threatened the very makeup of the Court by proposing to pack it with sympathetic justices who would go along with his counterrevolution. Although Roosevelt's plan failed, the justices had been effectively intimidated. And new justices, who shared Roosevelt's statism, began replacing older justices on the Court. It was not long before the Court became little more than a rubber stamp for Roosevelt's policies.

The federal government began passing laws and creating administrative agencies at a dizzying pace, increasing its control over economic activity and, hence, individual liberty. It used taxation not merely to fund constitutionally legitimate governmental activities, but also to redistribute wealth, finance welfare programs, set prices and production limits, create huge public works programs, and establish pension and unemployment programs. Roosevelt used his new power to expand political alliances and create electoral constituencies—unions, farmers, senior citizens, and ethnic groups. From this era forward, the Democratic Party and the federal government would become inextricably intertwined, and the Democratic Party would become as dependent on federal power for its sustenance as the governmental dependents it would create. Ironically, industrial expansion resulting from World War II eventually ended the Great Depression, not the New Deal. Indeed, the enormous tax and regulatory burden imposed on the private sector by the New Deal prolonged the economic recovery.

The significance of the New Deal is not in any one program, but in its sweeping break from our founding principles and constitutional limitations. Roosevelt himself broke with the two-presidential-term tradition started by George Washington by running for four terms. His legacy includes a federal government that has become a massive, unaccountable conglomerate: It is the nation's largest creditor, debtor, lender, employer, consumer, contractor, grantor, property owner, tenant, insurer, health-care provider, and pension guarantor.

And yet, the Statist has an insatiable appetite for control. His sights are set on his next meal even before he has fully digested his last. He is constantly agitating for government action. And in furtherance of that purpose, the Statist speaks in the tongue of the demagogue, concocting one pretext and grievance after another to manipulate public perceptions and build popular momentum for the divestiture of liberty and property from its rightful possessors. The industrious, earnest, and successful are demonized as perpetrators of various offenses against the public good, which justifies governmental intervention on behalf of an endless parade of "victims." In this way, the perpetrator and the victim are subordinated to the government's authority—the former by outright theft, the latter by a dependent existence. In truth, both are made victims by the real perpetrator, the Statist.

The Statist veils his pursuits in moral indignation, intoning in high dudgeon the injustices and inequities of liberty and life itself, for which only he can provide justice and bring a righteous resolution. And when the resolution proves elusive, as it undoubtedly does—whether the Marxist promise of "the workers' paradise" or the Great Society's "war on poverty"—the Statist demands ever more authority to wring out the imperfections of mankind's existence. Unconstrained by constitutional prohibitions, what is left to limit the Statist's ambitions but his own moral compass, which has already led him astray? He is never circumspect about his own shortcomings. Failure is not the product of his beliefs but merely want of power and resources. Thus are born endless rationalizations for seizing ever more governmental authority.

In the midst stands the individual, who was a predominate focus of the Founders. When living freely and pursuing his own legitimate interests, the individual displays qualities that are antithetical to the Statist's—initiative, self-reliance, and independence. As the Statist is building a culture of conformity and dependency, where the ideal citizen takes on dronelike qualities in service to the state, the individual must be drained of uniqueness and self-worth, and deterred from independent thought or behavior. This is achieved through varying methods of economic punishment and political suppression.

The Statist also knows that despite his successful usurpations, enough citizens are still skeptical and even distrustful of politicians and government that he cannot force his will all at once. Thus he marches in incremental steps, adjusting his pace as circumstances dictate. Today his pace is more rapid, for resistance has slowed. And at no time does the Statist do an about-face. But not so with some who claim the mantle of conservatism but are, in truth, neo-Statists, who would have the Conservative abandon the high ground of the founding principles for the quicksand of a soft tyranny.

Michael Gerson, formerly chief speechwriter for President George W. Bush, has written in his book, *Heroic Conservatism*, that "if Republicans run in future elections with a simplistic antigovernment message, ignoring the poor, the addicted and children at risk, they will lose, and they will deserve to lose." Gerson argues for a "compassionate conservatism" and "faith-based initiatives" in which the federal government plays a central role.[7]

Gerson all but ignores liberty's successes and the civil society in which humans flourish, even though he is surrounded in his

every moment by its magnificence. So numerous are liberty's trea-
sures that they defy cataloguing. The object of Gerson's scorn is
misplaced. Gerson does not ask, "How many enterprises and jobs
might have been created, how many people might have been
saved from illness and disease, how many more poor children
might have been fed but for the additional costs, market dislocations, and management inefficiencies that distort supply and demand or discourage research and development as a result of the
federal government's role?"

Liberty's permeance in American society often makes its man-
ifestations elusive or invisible to those born into it. Even if liberty
is acknowledged, it is often taken for granted and its permanence
assumed. Therefore, under these circumstances, the Statist's
agenda can be alluring even to a former advisor to a Republican
president. It is not recognized as an increasingly corrosive threat
to liberty but rather as coexisting with it.

Columnists William Kristol and David Brooks promote something called "national-greatness conservatism." They coauthored
an opinion piece in which they exclaimed that it "does not despise government. How could it? How can Americans love their
nation if they hate its government? But the way to restore faith in
our government is to slash its flabbiness while making it more effective."[8]

The Conservative does not despise government. He despises
tyranny. This is precisely why the Conservative reveres the Constitution and insists on adherence to it. An "effective" government that operates outside its constitutional limitations is a
dangerous government. By abandoning principle for efficiency,
the neo-Statist, it seems, is no more bound to the Constitution

than is the Statist. He marches more slowly than the Statist, but he marches with him nonetheless. The neo-Statist propounds no discernable standard or practical means to hem in the federal power he helps unleash, and which the Statist would exploit. In many ways, he is as objectionable as the Statist, for he seeks to devour conservatism by clothing himself in its nomenclature.

The Conservative is alarmed by the ascent of a soft tyranny and its cheery acceptance by the neo-Statist. He knows that liberty once lost is rarely recovered. He knows of the decline and eventual failure of past republics. And he knows that the best prescription for addressing society's real and perceived ailments is not to further empower an already enormous federal government beyond its constitutional limits, but to return to the founding principles. A free people living in a civil society, working in self-interested cooperation, and a government operating within the limits of its authority promote more prosperity, opportunity, and happiness for more people than any alternative. Conservatism is the antidote to tyranny precisely because its principles *are* the founding principles.

2

ON PRUDENCE AND PROGRESS

EVEN WHEN DECLARING INDEPENDENCE from England, the Founders recognized the dangers of imprudent change as it relates to governing. As the Declaration of Independence states,

> *That to secure these rights, Governments are instituted among Men, deriving their just powers from the consent of the governed, that whenever any Form of Government becomes destructive of these ends, it is the Right of the People to alter or to abolish it, and to institute new Government, laying its foundation on such principles and organizing its powers in such form, as to them shall seem most likely to effect their Safety and Happiness. Prudence, indeed, will dictate that Governments long established should not be changed for light and transient causes; and accordingly all experience hath shewn, that mankind are more disposed to suffer, while evils are sufferable, than to right themselves by abolishing the forms to which they are accus-*

tomed. But when a long train of abuses and usurpations, pursu-
ing invariably the same Object evinces a design to reduce them
under absolute Despotism, it is their right, it is their duty, to
throw off such Government, and to provide new Guards for
their future security. . . .

The Founders were very careful to explain that revolution is a last resort compelled only by the imposition of an absolute despotism. No right-thinking Conservative today would encourage overthrowing the United States government, for he does not toil under the iron fist of absolute despotism, even though the Conservative is alarmed at the Statist's growing success in substituting arbitrary state power for ordered liberty.

However, the Conservative does not reject change. Edmund Burke wrote that "a state without the means of some change is without the means of its conservation."[1] What kind of change, then, does the Conservative support?

Burke explained,

There is a manifest, marked distinction, which ill men with ill
designs, or weak men incapable of any design, will constantly
be confounding,—that is, a marked distinction between change
and reformation. The former alters the substance of the objects
themselves, and gets rid of all their essential good as well as of
all the accidental evil annexed to them. Change is novelty; and
whether it is to operate any one of the effects of reformation at
all, or whether it may not contradict the very principle upon
which reformation is desired, cannot be known beforehand. Re-
form is not change in the substance or in the primary modifica-

tion of the object, but a direct application of a remedy to the grievance complained of. So far as that is removed, all is sure. It stops there; and if it fails, the substance which underwent the operation, at the very worst, is but where it was.[2]

For Burke, change as reform was intended to preserve and improve the basic institutions of the state. Change as innovation was destructive as a radical departure from the past and the substitution of existing institutions of the state with potentially dangerous experiments.[3] Furthermore, the Statist often justifies change as conferring new, abstract rights, which is nothing more than a Statist deception intended to empower the state and deny man his real rights—those that are both unalienable and anchored in custom, tradition, and faith. Burke wrote, "By this unprincipled facility of changing the state as often, and as much, and in as many ways, as there are floating fancies or fashions, the whole chain and continuity of the commonwealth would be broken. No one generation could link with the other. Men would become little better than the flies of a summer."[4]

The Conservative believes, as Burke and the Founders did, that prudence must be exercised in assessing change. *Prudence is the highest virtue for it is judgment drawn on wisdom.* The proposed change should be informed by the experience, knowledge, and traditions of society, tailored for a specific purpose, and accomplished through a constitutional construct that ensures thoughtful deliberation by the community. Change unconstrained by prudence produces unpredictable consequences, threatening ordered liberty with chaos and ultimately despotism, and placing at risk the very principles the Conservative holds dear.

However, the Conservative seeks to preserve and improve the civil society, not engage in a mindless defense of the status quo inasmuch as the status quo may well be a condition created by the Statist and destructive of the civil society—such as 1960s cultural degradations, which are all too prevalent today. It is the Statist, then, who rejects even minor change if such change promotes the civil society, thereby challenging his authority.

The Conservative understands that Americans are living in a state of diminishing liberty—that statism is on the ascendancy and the societal balance is tipping away from ordered liberty. In these circumstances, the Conservative should not confuse prudence with timidity. If anything, certainly since the New Deal, the Conservative has too often lacked the confidence and persistence to defend the civil society.

Even the most dedicated Conservative acknowledges, however, the daunting challenge ahead. The Founders were right when they observed that man has a high tolerance for suffering.

The Conservative must accept that the Statist does not share his passion for liberty and all the good that flows from it. The Statist does not acknowledge the tremendous benefits to society from the individual pursuits of tens of millions of others. The Statist rejects the Founders' idea of the dignity of the individual, who can flourish through ordered liberty, for one rooted in unpredictability, irrationality and, ultimately, tyranny.

It is observed that the Statist is dissatisfied with the condition of his own existence. He condemns his fellow man, surroundings, and society itself for denying him the fulfillment, success, and adulation he believes he deserves. He is angry, resentful, petulant, and jealous. He is incapable of honest self-assessment and rejects the honest assessment by others of himself, thereby evading responsibility for his own miserable condition. The Statist searches for significance and even glory in a utopian fiction of his mind's making, the earthly attainment of which, he believes, is frustrated by those who do not share it. Therefore, he must destroy the civil society, piece by piece.

For the Statist, liberty is not a blessing but the enemy. It is not possible to achieve Utopia if individuals are free to go their own way. The individual must be dehumanized and his nature delegitimized. Through persuasion, deception, and coercion, the individual must be subordinated to the state. He must abandon his own ambitions for the ambitions of the state. He must become reliant on and fearful of the state. His first duty must be to the state—not family, community, and faith, all of which have the potential of threatening the state. Once dispirited, the individual can be molded by the state.

The Statist's Utopia can take many forms, and has throughout human history, including monarchism, feudalism, militarism, fascism, communism, national socialism, and economic socialism. They are all of the same species—tyranny. The primary principle around which the Statist organizes can be summed up in a single word—*equality*.

Equality, as understood by the Founders, is the natural right of every individual to live freely under self-government, to acquire and retain the property he creates through his own labor, and to be treated impartially before a just law. Moreover, equality should not be confused with perfection, for man is also imperfect, making his application of equality, even in the most just society, imperfect. Otherwise, inequality is the natural state of man in the sense that each individual is born unique in all his human characteristics. Therefore, equality and inequality, properly comprehended, are both engines of liberty.

The Statist, however, misuses equality to pursue uniform economic and social outcomes. He must continuously enhance his power at the expense of self-government and violate the individual's property rights at the expense of individual liberty, for he believes that through persuasion, deception, and coercion he can tame man's natural state and man's perfection can, therefore, be achieved in Utopia. The Statist must claim the power to make that which is unequal equal and that which is imperfect perfect. This is the hope the Statist offers, if only the individual surrenders himself to the all-powerful state. Only then can the impossible be made possible.

President Barack Obama made this point when lecturing the Wesleyan University graduating class of 2008 during his campaign: "[O]ur individual salvation depends on collective salvation."[5] But salvation is not government's to give. Indeed, it is not a grant to mankind from mankind. Under the wrong conditions and in the wrong hands, this deviant view is a powerful tool against humanity. The difficulty if not impossibility is in containing the soft tyranny so it does not metastasize into a more absolute tyranny, since the diminished and then vanquished civil society is the sole anecdote.

American history and traditions make the transformation from civil society to tyranny more complicated for the Statist than in Europe and other places, which helps explain its slower pace. As French philosopher Raymond Aron wrote in 1955, "[In America] there is no sign of either the traditions or the classes which give European ideas their meaning. Aristocracy, and the aristocratic way of life, were ruthlessly eliminated by the War of Independence."[6] Still, tyranny is a threat that looms over all societies, preventable only by the active vigilance of the people. The Statist in America is no less resolute than his European counterpart but, by necessity, he is more cunning—where the European lurches and leaps, the American's steps are measured but steady. In America, the Statist understands that his counterrevolution must at least appear gradual and not revolutionary—sometimes even clothed in the flag and patriotism—lest his intentions become too obvious and thus alarming to his skeptics.

For the Statist, the international community and international organizations serve as useful sources for importing disaffection with the civil society. The Statist urges Americans to view themselves through the lenses of those who resent and even hate them. He needs Americans to become less confident, to doubt their institutions, and to accept the status assigned to them by outsiders—as isolationists, invaders, occupiers, oppressors, and exploiters. The Statist wants Americans to see themselves as backward, foolishly holding to their quaint notions of individual liberty, private property, family, and faith, long diminished or jettisoned in other countries. They need to listen to the voices of condemnation from world capitals and self-appointed global watchdogs hostile to America's superior standard of living. America is said to be out of step and regressive, justifying the surrendering of its sovereignty through treaties and other arrangements that benefit the greater "humanity." And it would not hurt if America admitted its past transgressions, made reparations, and accepted its fate as just another aging nation—one among many.

The Statist must also rely on legions of academics to serve as his missionaries. After a short period of training and observation, academics receive a sinecure—a personal stake in the state via lifetime employment through a system of tenure. The classroom is turned into a propaganda mill, rather than a place for education, to shape the beliefs and attitudes of successive generations of malcontents and incubate the quiet revolution against the civil society. Academics help identify the enemies of the state, whom their students learn to distrust or even detest through distortion and repetition—corporations as polluters, the Founding Fathers as slave owners, the military as imperialist, etc.

Academics claim to challenge authority but, in truth, preach authoritarianism through various justifications for and approaches to deconstructing the civil society. They talk of individual rights but promote collectivism. They talk of enfranchisement and suffrage but promote judicial and administrative usurpation of republicanism. They talk of workers' rights but promote the heavy taxation and regulation of labor. Indeed, academics portray Utopia as a kind of heaven on earth but have a high tolerance for the hell of widespread misery. The academic knows from history, and better than most, the destructive power of the Statist's way. But he believes it is the price humanity must pay to pave the way for Utopia—or, conversely, he dismisses Statist-caused misery as a misapplication of utopian ideals resulting from the poor performance of a particular Statist or the nefarious doings of the enemies of the state.

The academy's first cousin is Hollywood, which uses entertainment to besmirch the civil society. Why would actors who are celebrated for freely practicing their profession do the Statist's bidding?

Writing not just of actors but all those who "pretend to themselves that they are still pushing envelopes and slashing away at bourgeois complacency," University of Tennessee professor Wilfred M. McClay observes, "There is profound self-deception at work in people who luxuriate in the fruits of worldly success while disdaining the personal habits and cultural conditions that make such success possible. There is also a strangely hidden compulsion behind the need for such condemnation. Yet somehow even the most incongruous social conventions can take hold for a time, and in our era, the conjunction of a dutiful other-directedness with a dutiful rebelliousness seems by now so entrenched and commonplace as to be almost natural. Its existence would make it very challenging to be *truly* countercultural if one is of a mind to be."[7]

The late Eric Hoffer, the blue-collar philosopher, provides a compelling answer: "Those who see their lives as spoiled and wasted crave equality and fraternity more than they do freedom. If they clamor for freedom, it is but freedom to establish equality and uniformity. The passion for equality is partly a passion for anonymity: to be one thread of the many which make up a tunic; one thread not distinguishable from the others. No one can then point us out, measure us against others and expose our inferiority."[8]

The actor thirsts for attention. But he lives in the world of make-believe. Once he achieves fame, he wishes for his fame to be used to achieve relevance. Attention and fame would appear to be at odds with anonymity, but the actor finds anonymity in the larger fraternity that is Hollywood and relevance in its causes—Marxism in the 1940s to global warming today. It is the rare actor who challenges the fraternity.

The Statist is also assisted by the media, for the media are parasites of the Statist—not the government per se but the Statist. They gather information produced by the Statist and regurgitate it to the masses. The relationship between the Statist and media is symbiotic. The Statist protects the media and enhances the media's clout by censoring the speech of others, usually at the insistence of the media. Today, campaign finance laws restrict the amount of resources individuals can use to speak about candidates to their fellow citizens during political contests. And even if the necessary resources are raised, the Statist prohibits their use for broadcast communications in the crucial days running up to the election. Hence, the individual must rely inordinately on the media for disseminating information.

To the extent there are pockets of independence that challenge the Statist, they are treated like tumors that need to be isolated and excised to achieve the purity of the body politic. There are current efforts to resuscitate the so-called Fairness Doctrine and similar connivances—which would circumscribe the content of speech on talk radio—simply because the forum is generally hostile to the Statist.[9] The media decry alternative information outlets on the Internet, which do not vet their content through the media's editors. There are now rumblings about regulating the Internet, which occurs in places like China. Of course, these neutering strategies are said by the Statist to actually promote speech, or responsible speech, thereby disguising his real motives.[10]

The media sing like a nay-saying Greek chorus, amplifying the mantra for greater statist authority. No matter how robust the economy, they claim the imminent threat of a recession or depression. And when economic hardship exists, often at the hand of the Statist, they join the Statist in condemning the free market and advocating for more government. No matter the progress in race relations, they insist racism is rampant. In the weeks leading up to the election of President Barack Obama, the media reported repeatedly of the racist citizens who would deny Obama his victory should he lose. No matter the advances of the health-care system, the media paint it as inferior to all others, with anecdotal stories of incompetence and services denied to help promote statist health-care proposals. Rarely do the media report of the nightmarish, systemic failures of the British or Canadian national health-care experiments. For the most part the Statist's enemies are the media's enemies, as reflected in their hostility to individuality and private property, and the Statist and the media have kindred spirits in academia and Hollywood. Their effect is to soften up the population to become receptive to the counterrevolution—or at least lessen resistance to it.

Support for the Statist ought not be confused with support for the state as is. The Statist himself will criticize the state, not for the purpose of reforming it or reducing it, but for changing it in the name of reforming it. The counterrevolution is a constant revolution, since the Statist can never rid the individual or state of imperfection and inequality, no matter how hard he tries. He is obsessed with the task nonetheless and is credited with deep compassion for the effort.

The British writer-philosopher C. S. Lewis wrote, "Of all tyrannies, a tyranny sincerely exercised for the good of its victims may be the most oppressive. It would be better to live under rob-ber barons than under omnipotent moral busybodies. The robber baron's cruelty may sometimes sleep, his cupidity may at some point be satiated; but those who torment us for our own good will torment us without end for they do so with the approval of their own conscience."[11]

3

ON FAITH AND THE FOUNDING

REASON CANNOT, BY ITSELF, explain why there is reason. Science cannot, by itself, explain why there is science. Man's discovery and application of science are products of reason.

Reason and science can explain the existence of matter, but they cannot explain why there is matter. They can explain the existence of the universe, but they cannot explain why there is a universe. They can explain the existence of nature and the law of physics, but they cannot explain why there is nature and the law of physics. They can explain the existence of life, but they cannot explain why there is life. They can explain the existence of consciousness, but they cannot explain why there is consciousness.[1]

Science is a critical aspect of human existence, but it cannot address the spiritual nature of man. In this respect, science is a dead end around which the Atheist refuses to reason. Reason itself informs man of its own limitations and, in doing so, directs him to the discovery of a force greater than himself—a supernatural force responsible for the origins of not only human existence but all existence, and which itself has always existed and will always exist. For most, the supernatural reveals itself in the Creator—God. Man seeks God's guidance through faith and prayer. The Agnostic accepts the supernatural, but is not so sure of the form of its existence. The Deist accepts that God created the universe and man's condition but left it to man to sort things out through reason.

Man is more than a physical creature. As Edmund Burke argued, each individual is created as a unique, spiritual being with a soul and a conscience and is bound to a transcendent moral order established by Divine Providence and uncovered through observation and experience over the ages.[2] "There is but one law for all, namely, that law which governs all law, the law of our Creator, the law of humanity, justice, equity—the law of nature and of nations."[3] This is the Natural Law that penetrates man's being and which the Founding Fathers adopted as the principle around which civilized American society would be organized.

The Declaration of Independence appeals to "the Laws of Nature and of Nature's God." It provides further, "We hold these truths to be self-evident, that all men are created equal, that they are *endowed by their Creator* with certain unalienable Rights, that among these are Life, Liberty, and the pursuit of Happiness."

The Founders were enlightened men, but not men purely of the Age of Enlightenment. They were highly educated, well-informed men who excelled at reason and subscribed to science but worshiped neither. They comprehended them—their strengths as well as weaknesses. The Declaration's signers were Congregationalist, Presbyterian, Anglican, Unitarian, and Roman Catholic. At least two Founders, Thomas Jefferson and Benjamin Franklin, are widely believed to have been Deists. They were men of varying denominations but united and emphatic in the belief that the Creator was the origin of their existence and the source of their reason.

Is it possible that there is no Natural Law and man can know moral order and unalienable rights from his own reasoning, unaided by the supernatural or God? There are, of course, those who argue this case—including the Atheist and others who attempt to distinguish Natural Law from Divine Providence. It is not the view adopted by the Founders. This position would, it seems, lead man to arbitrarily create his own morality and rights, or create his own arbitrary morality and rights—right and wrong, just and unjust, good and bad, would be relative concepts susceptible to circumstantial applications. Moreover, by what justification would "Life, Liberty, and the pursuit of Happiness" be "unalienable Rights" if there is no Natural Law, since reason alone cannot make them inviolable? What then is Natural Law if its origin is unknown or rejected? It is nothing more than a human construct. An individual may benefit from the moral order and unalienable rights around which society functions while rejecting their Divine origin. But the civil society cannot organize itself that way. It would become unstable and vulnerable to anarchy and tyranny, imperiling all within it, especially the individual. The abandonment of Natural Law is the adoption of tyranny in one form or another, because there is no humane or benevolent alternative to Natural Law.

Some resist the idea of Natural Law's relationship to Divine Providence, for they fear it leads to intolerance or even theocracy.

They have that backwards. If man is "endowed by [the] Creator with certain unalienable rights," he is endowed with these rights no matter his religion or whether he has allegiance to any religion. It is Natural Law, divined by God and discoverable by reason, that prescribes the inalienability of the most fundamental and eternal human rights—rights that are not conferred on man by man and, therefore, cannot legitimately be denied to man by man. It is the Divine nature of Natural Law that makes permanent man's right to "Life, Liberty, and the pursuit of Happiness." In the last sentence of the Declaration, the Founders proclaimed: "And for the support of this Declaration, with a firm reliance on the protection of *Divine Providence*, we mutually pledge to each other our Lives, our Fortunes, and our sacred Honor."

And what of the government's role in religion, or vice versa? Prior to the founding, America was a land settled by people mostly from Europe, and many of them were escaping religious persecution. Consequently, several colonies had distinct religious and denominational characteristics. The Puritans (and later Baptists and Congregationalists) were concentrated in New England, the Quakers in Pennsylvania, the Roman Catholics in Maryland, etc. Several of the colonies were immersed in religion, some more than others, and some were more tolerant of religious diversity than others. Many settlers were drawn to America in search of economic opportunity and congregated in places such as New York, New Jersey, and Georgia.

In 1776, when representatives of the colonies signed the Declaration, they did so for the first time as representatives of *states* and as part of a loose confederation. The designation of the colonies as states did not erase the long histories and traditions of the former colonies. Many continued to promote religion with taxes and land grants. Some states required officials to affirm their allegiance to a particular religion or religious sect by way of an oath, although this practice was dropped a few decades after the founding. And some states continued to discriminate against certain religions. But when they bound themselves to the Declaration's principles, they bound themselves to, among other things, religious liberty. It is little understood that the Declaration was a declaration of political *and* religious liberty.

Despite its different denominations, Christianity was and is America's dominant religion. There is no dispute that Judeo-Christian values and traditions have and do influence America's fundamental laws and policies. However, despite its varying practices and applications in the colonies and the early years of the states, Christianity itself does not preach operational dominance over the body politic or seek justification from it, even while it promotes and defends its teachings through proselytism and activism. In contrasting Christianity to Islam in this respect, Alexis de Tocqueville observed that "Mohammed professed to derive from Heaven, and he has inserted in the Koran, not only a body of religious doctrines, but political maxims, civil and criminal laws, and theories of science. The Gospel, on the contrary, only speaks of the general relations of men to God and to each other— beyond which it inculcates and imposes no point of faith. . . ."[4]

In Saudi Arabia, the Basic Law provides that "the nation's constitution consists of the Quran and the Sunna, the actions and sayings of the prophet as recorded in the Hadith. . . . [S]upreme religious councils dictate how Islamic law is applied and, to a large extent, have veto power over legislation."[5] Islamic law, or *sharia*, dictates the most intricate aspects of daily life, from politics and finance to dating and hygiene. There is not, and never has been, support for a national construct of this sort in America.

The Constitution's Framers wrote the First Amendment to include the words "Congress shall make no law respecting an establishment of religion, or prohibiting the free exercise thereof . . ." *because* they believed the establishment of a theocracy would be destructive of both liberty generally *and* religious liberty in particular. Although the First Amendment, as originally intended and applied, had no effect on the states, its adoption by the federal Congress and ratification by the states evinced a national consensus that liberty and religious liberty are inseparable, the same national consensus that motivated the Declaration's signers. The Founders were remarkably foresighted. It is no accident that Americans are among the most religious and tolerant people in the world.

For the Statist, however, the Declaration is an impediment to his schemes. The Statist cannot abide the existence of Natural Law and man's discovery of "unalienable rights" bestowed on all individuals by "their Creator." In ideology and practice, the Statist believes rights are not a condition of man's existence but only exist to the extent the Statist ratifies them. Furthermore, rights do not belong to all individuals. They are to be rationed by the state—conferred on those whom the Statist believes deserving of them, and denied to those whom the Statist believes undeserving of them. He acknowledges only that law which he himself sets in place, and which is subject to change or arbitrary application on his say-so. The Statist may wrap himself and his deeds in the language of enlightenment—claiming to be the voice of reason, the beholder of knowledge, and the architect of modernity—but recent history has shown him to be unenlightened in his understanding of mankind, moral order, liberty, and equality. Statists have launched bloody revolutions followed by violent periods of terror in France, Russia, Germany, China, and elsewhere, always under the flags of democratic populism, Marxism, national socialism, and fascism. For the Statist, revolution is an ongoing enterprise, for it regularly cleanses society of religious dogma, antiquated traditions, backward customs, and ambitious individuals who differ with or obstruct the Statist's plans. The Statist calls this many things, including "progressive." For the rest, it is tyranny.

Is the Statist a Secularist, or vice versa? The Secularist may believe in the supernatural or God and practice a religion but share the Statist's objective of excluding their influence from public life. If such a Secularist also shares the Statist's egalitarian ends, he is at one with the Statist—a religious Statist or a Secular religionist, if you will—oddly endorsing the Enlightenment without Natural Law and the Statist's promise of heaven on earth. Moreover, the Statist may express his politics in the semantics of religion to disarm religious believers and enlist their support to simultaneously advance his secular and, ultimately, statist agenda. A Secularist may also be a Statist stripped of God or religion.

It is no coincidence that with the rise of New Deal statism, secularism would rise with it. It is also unsurprising that secularism would make its strongest showing not from the ranks of the people's representatives, but from the judiciary.

In 1947, in the case *Everson v. Board of Education*, Associate Supreme Court Justice Hugo Black, writing for a 5–4 majority, asserted that "no tax in any amount, large or small, can be levied to support any religious activities or institutions, whatever they may be called, or whatever form they may adopt to teach or practice religion."[6] He added, "The First Amendment has erected a wall between church and state. That wall must be kept high and impregnable. We could not approve the slightest breach."[7]

Black had been Franklin Roosevelt's first appointee to the Supreme Court. He was a senator from Alabama—and a reliable New Deal proponent in the Senate and on the Court. He had also been a member of the Ku Klux Klan in the 1920s and was hostile toward the Catholic Church. According to Black's son, "The Ku Klux Klan and Daddy, so far as I could tell, had one thing in common. He suspected the Catholic Church. He used to read all of Paul Blanshard's books exposing the power abuse in the Catholic Church. He thought the Pope and the bishops had too much power and property. He resented the fact that rental property owned by the Church was not taxed; he felt they got most of their revenue from the poor and did not return enough of it."[8]

Whatever Black's motivations, he orchestrated a wretched betrayal of America's founding and succeeded in rewriting the First Amendment to say what the Framers would never have countenanced.

Chief Justice William Rehnquist argued in 1985, in the case *Wallace v. Jaffree*, "The [First Amendment's] Establishment Clause did not require government neutrality between religion and irreligion nor did it prohibit the Federal Government from providing nondiscriminatory aid to religion. There is simply no historical foundation for the proposition that the Framers intended to build a 'wall of separation' that was constitutionalized in *Everson*."[9]

Actually, the Founders did not require nondiscriminatory aid to religion, for it existed at the time of the founding and the Constitution's ratification. They rejected the establishment of a national religion, leaving the states free to make their own decisions. And by the time *Everson* was decided, the few states that had established churches had long past abolished them. Still, the *Everson* fiat applied to all levels of government because the Court was not concerned with the establishment of a theocracy but rather with establishing a secular polity. And the courts subsequently extended *Everson* to mean the exclusion of references to God in certain public settings. A more thorough repudiation of the nation's founding principles—of Natural Law and God-given unalienable rights—would be difficult to invent. Indeed, as Claremont Institute senior fellow and University of Dallas professor Thomas G. West wrote, "[T]he Supreme Court will allow the theology of the Declaration to be taught in the classroom as long as it is understood that it belongs to a 'world that is dead and gone,' that it has nothing to do with the world that we live in here and now, that it is not a living faith that holds God to be the source of our rights, the author of the laws of nature, and the protector and Supreme Judge of America."[10]

A theocracy is not established if certain public schools allow their students to pray at the beginning of the day, or participate in Christmas or Easter assemblies; or if certain school districts transport parochial students to their religious schools as part of the district's bus route; or certain communities choose to construct a manger scene on the grounds of their town hall or display the Ten

Commandments above their courthouse steps. The individual is not required to change his religious affiliation or even accept God's existence. He is not required to worship against his beliefs or even worship at all. Some might be uncomfortable or offended by these events, but individuals are uncomfortable all the time over all kinds of government activities. Some might oppose the use of their tax dollars to support these events. So what? Individuals oppose the manner in which government uses their tax dollars all the time. That does not make the uses unconstitutional. While all religions may not have similar access to these public places, they are largely free to conduct themselves as they wish, uninhibited by the community, as long as they do not engage in criminal or immoral practices. Yet even these *passive* expressions of religious liberty, which represent a community's dominant religion or religious denomination, must, according to the Secularist and the Court, be abandoned.

The American courts sit today as supreme secular councils, which, like Islam's supreme religious councils, dictate all manner of approved behavior respecting religion. Whereas the supreme religious councils enforce Islamic law, the supreme secular councils have seized for themselves the mission of segregating God and religion from public life and have immersed themselves in religious matters. Neither of the councils tolerates conflicting or diverse viewpoints, insisting that their rulings are the final word for all society.

The question must be asked and answered: Is it possible for the Conservative to be a Secularist? There are conservatives who self-identify as secularists, whether or not they believe in God or take a religion, and it is not for others to deny them their personal beliefs. However, it must be observed that the Declaration is at opposite with the Secularist. Therefore, the Conservative would be no less challenged than any other to make coherent that which is irreconcilable.

Moreover, for the Conservative, as it was for Burke and the Founders, faith is not a threat to civil society but rather vital to its survival. It encourages the individual to personally adhere to a dogma that promotes restraint, duty, and moral behavior, which not only benefit the individual but the multitudes and society generally. As George Washington wrote in his Farewell Address, "Of all the dispositions and habits which lead to political prosperity, religion and morality are indispensable results. . . . And let us with caution indulge the supposition that morality can be maintained without religion." [11]

Attempts to stigmatize as "religious zealots" or marginalize as "social extremists" those individuals who resist the Statist's secular impositions—for they are the coercion behind America's moral and cultural decline—is to condemn conservatism, the Founders, and the civil society. How can it be said, as it often is, that moral order is second to liberty when one cannot survive without the other? A people cannot remain free and civilized without moral purposes, constraints, and duties. What would be left but relativism manifesting itself in anarchy, followed by tyranny and brute force? For the Conservative, "social issues" relating to life and lifestyle, tested by human experience through the centuries, are not merely personal habits and beliefs but also merit encouragement throughout the society.

In his 1964 speech accepting the Republican nomination for president, Senator Barry Goldwater declared that "those who elevate the state and downgrade the citizen must see ultimately a world in which earthly power can be substituted for Divine Will, and this Nation was founded upon the rejection of that notion and upon the acceptance of God as the author of freedom."[12] While in his later years Goldwater denounced certain proselytes, in this, his most important speech, his call to God's will and the founding—linking one to the other—could not have been more unequivocal.

4

ON THE CONSTITUTION

LANGUAGE CONSISTS OF WORDS, words have ordinary and common meanings, and those meanings are communicated to others through the written and spoken word. When parties enter into voluntary arrangements, such as contracts, they use words to describe the terms and conditions by which they are obligated to perform and on which they are expected to rely. Contracts are interpreted, and the intentions of the parties discerned, in the context of their original making.

The Conservative is an *originalist*, for he believes that much like a contract, the Constitution sets forth certain terms and conditions for governing that hold the same meaning today as they did yesterday and should tomorrow. It connects one generation to the next by restraining the present generation from societal experimentation and government excess. There really is no other standard by which the Constitution can be interpreted without abandoning its underlying principles altogether.

If the Constitution's meaning can be erased or rewritten, and the Framers' intentions ignored, it ceases to be a constitution but is instead a concoction of political expedients that serve the contemporary policy agendas of the few who are entrusted with public authority to preserve it.

As James Madison, the "father" of the Constitution, explained:

> *I entirely concur in the propriety of resorting to the sense in which the Constitution was accepted and ratified by the nation. In that sense alone it is the legitimate Constitution. And if that be not the guide in expounding it, there can be no security for a consistent and stable, more than for a faithful exercise of its powers. If the meaning of the text be sought in the changeable meaning of the words composing it, it is evident that the shapes and attributes of the Government must partake of the changes to which the words and phrases of all living languages are constantly subject. What a metamorphosis would be produced in the code of law if all its ancient phraseology were to be taken in its modern sense. And that the language of our Constitution is already undergoing interpretations unknown to its founders, will I believe appear to all unbiased Enquirers into the history of its origin and adoption.[1]*

To say that the Constitution is a "living and breathing document" is to give license to arbitrary and lawless activism. It is a mantra that gained purchase in the early twentieth century and is paraded around by the Statist as if to legitimate that which is illegitimate.[2]

Thomas Jefferson, in an 1803 letter to Senator Wilson Cary

Nicholas of Virginia respecting the Louisiana Purchase, explained:

> *Our peculiar security is in possession of a written Constitution. Let us not make it a blank paper by construction. I say the same as to the opinion of those who consider the grant of the treaty-making power as boundless. If it is, then we have no Constitution. If it has bounds, they can be no others than the definitions of the powers which that instrument gives. It specifies & delineates the operations permitted to the federal government, and gives all the powers necessary to carry these into execution. Whatever of these enumerated objects is proper for a law, Congress may make the law; whatever is proper to be executed by way of a treaty, the President & Senate may enter into the treaty; whatever is to be done by a judicial sentence, the judges may pass the sentence.*[3]

The Constitution is the bedrock on which a living, evolving nation was built. It is—and must be—a timeless yet durable foundation that individuals can count on in a changing world. It is not perfect but the Framers made it more perfectible through the amendment process.

The Conservative seeks to divine the Constitution's meaning from its words and their historical context, including a variety of original sources—records of public debates, diaries, correspondence, notes, etc. While reasonable people may, in good faith, draw different conclusions from the application of this interpretative standard, it is the only standard that gives fidelity to the Constitution.

And where the Constitution is silent, states and individuals need not be. The Constitution and, more particularly, the framework of the government it establishes are not intended to address every issue or answer every perceived grievance. This is not a defect but a strength, because the government was intended to be a limited one.[4]

The Statist is not interested in what the Framers said or intended. He is interested only in what *he* says and *he* intends. Consider the judiciary, which has seized for itself the most dominant role in interpreting the Constitution. When asked by a law clerk to explain his judicial philosophy, the late Associate Supreme Court justice Thurgood Marshall responded, "You do what you think is *right* and let the law catch up."[5] The late Associate justice Arthur Goldberg's answer was no better. A law clerk recounts Goldberg telling him that his approach was to determine "what is the *just* result."[6] Still others are persuaded by the Statist's semantic distortions, arguing that the judge's job is to spread *democracy*[7] or *liberty*.[8]

The Conservative may ask the following questions: If words and their meaning can be manipulated or ignored to advance the Statist's political and policy preferences, what then binds allegiance to the Statist's words? Why should today's law bind future generations if yesterday's law does not bind this generation? Why should judicial precedent bind the nation if the Constitution itself does not? Why should any judicial determination based on a judge's notion of what is "right" or "just" bind the individual if the individual believes the notion is wrong and unjust? Does not lawlessness beget lawlessness? Or is not the Statist really saying that the law is what he says it is, and that is the beginning and end of it? And if judges determine for society what is right and just, and if their purpose is to spread democracy or liberty, how can it be said that the judiciary is coequal with the executive or legislative branch?

The Statist considers the judiciary his clearest path to amassing authority, for through it he can proclaim what the law is without effective challenge or concern with the fleeting outcome of an election cycle. Moreover, the federal judiciary is populated with about one thousand lawyers—and the Supreme Court a mere nine—making statist infiltration easy. Even when holding high office in the executive or legislative branches, the Statist today looks for ways to enhance judicial authority at the expense of his own branch, for in doing so he seeks to immunize his agenda from a possible change in public attitudes. And the Statist on the Court tolerates representative government only to the extent that its decisions reinforce his ends. Otherwise, he overrules it.

There was a time when Franklin Roosevelt, the Statist's favorite president, was an Originalist who respected the Constitution's wise formulations and purpose. In 1930, as governor of New York, he delivered a speech condemning "the doctrine of regulation by 'master minds,' in whose judgment and will all the people may gladly and quietly acquiesce. . . . Were it possible to find 'master minds' so unselfish, so willing to decide unhesitatingly against their own personal interests or private prejudices, men almost god-like in their ability to hold the scales of Justice with an even hand, such a government might be to the interest of the country, but there are none such on our political horizon, and we cannot expect a complete reversal of all the teachings of history."[9] He added, "Now, to bring about government by oligarchy masquerading as democracy, it is fundamentally essential that practically all authority and control be centralized in our National Government."[10]

But, alas, Roosevelt went on to become the very "master mind" he had denounced earlier in his political career. In his 1944 State of the Union address to Congress, Roosevelt declared, "This Republic had its beginning, and grew to its present strength, under the protection of certain inalienable rights—among them the right of free speech, free press, free worship, trial by jury, freedom from unreasonable searches and seizures. They were our rights to life and liberty."[11] But for Roosevelt, these rights were no longer enough. He went on to propose a "Second Bill of Rights" based on "security and prosperity."[12]

> The right to a useful and remunerative job in the industries or shops or farms or mines of the Nation; to earn enough to provide adequate food and clothing and recreation; of every farmer to raise and sell his products at a return which will give him and his family a decent living; of every businessman, large and small, to trade in an atmosphere of freedom from unfair competition and domination by monopolies at home or abroad; of every family to a decent home; to adequate medical care and the opportunity to achieve and enjoy good health; to adequate protection from the economic fears of old age, sickness, accident, and unemployment; to a good education.[13]

This is tyranny's disguise. These are not rights. They are the Statist's false promises of utopianism, which the Statist uses to justify all trespasses on the individual's private property. Liberty and private property go hand in hand. By dominating one the Statist dominates both, for if the individual cannot keep or dispose of the value he creates by his own intellectual and/or physical labor, he exists to serve the state. The "Second Bill of Rights" and its legal and policy progeny require the individual to surrender control of his fate to the government.

And there is a movement afoot among the professoriate to compel exactly that result—not through the ballot box, but by constitutional deviation.

Georgetown University law professor Robin West argues that "[w]e need . . . a progressive jurisprudence—a jurisprudence that embraces rather than resists, and then reinterprets, our liberal commitment to the 'rule of law,' the content of our individual rights, and the dream of formal equality. More inclusive interpretations—more generous reimaginings—could then undergird, and in a principled way, particular constitutional arguments. Rather than relentlessly buck, deconstruct and vilify the seeming 'naturalness' of legal arguments based on moral premises, we ought to be providing such premises, and natural and general arguments of our own. But first we need to re-imagine."[14] She has also promoted the view that the Fourteenth Amendment's equal protection clause delegitimizes social and economic inequality.[15] Yale law professor Bruce Ackerman says his "aim is to redeem the lost promise of the Fourteenth Amendment's vision of national citizenship through the enactment of framework statutes and the judicial development of the meaning of 'privileges' and 'immunities' of American citizenship."[16]

Here is what the relevant part of the Fourteenth Amendment actually says:

All persons born or naturalized in the United States and subject
to the jurisdiction thereof, are citizens of the United States and
of the State wherein they reside. No State shall make or enforce
any law which shall abridge the privileges or immunities of citi-
zens of the United States; nor shall any State deprive any per-
son of life, liberty, or property, without due process of law; nor
deny to any person within its jurisdiction the equal protection of
the laws.[17]

No literate person can comprehend the Fourteenth Amendment to mean what the Statists in academia claim it to mean.
The Fourteenth Amendment was intended to grant African-
Americans the same rights that exist for all Americans, not to
install the wholly foreign regimen of economic and social egali-
tarianism.[18] The Statist willfully distorts not only the Framers'
intent in adopting the Constitution, but the actions of subsequent
Congresses and state legislatures in amending the Constitution.

And these are the academic communities from which future
judges are groomed and plucked.

By now it should be clear that the debate over constitutional
interpretation is a false one. The Statist is not interpreting but
manipulating. As Ackerman has said, "The progressive vision of
frameworks centers on the economy—[it] needs to be constitutionalized in frameworks to make real the notion of a common
citizenship."[19] Hence, the Statist's agenda would be constitutionally mandated, leaving the representative branches and, ultimately, the people, no way to escape it.

Former Harvard University law professor and current Obama
administration official Cass Sunstein, a leading advocate of

delinking liberty and property rights—and President Barack Obama's likely future nominee to the Supreme Court—considers Roosevelt's "Second Bill of Rights" to be among his greatest speeches. It is, therefore, important that some attention be paid to Sunstein.

Sunstein believes that economic value and private property are not natural occurrences in human interaction but rather the outgrowth of government and law. Therefore, he and other legal "realists" assert that government authority should be used to better exploit and redistribute wealth. As Sunstein explains:

> [I]f some people have a lot and others little, law and legal coercion is a large part of the reason. Of course many people work hard and many others do not. But the distribution of wealth is not simply a product of hard work; it depends on a coercive network of legal rights and obligations. The realists complained that we ignore the extent to which we have what we have and do what we do because of the law. They contended that people tend to see as "voluntary" and "free" interactions that are shot through with public force. In their view, the laws of property, contract and tort are social creations that allocate certain rights to some people and deny them to others. These forms of law represent large-scale government "interventions" into the economy. They are coercive to the extent that they prohibit people from engaging in desired activities. If homeless people lack a place to live, it is not because of God's will or nature. It is because the rules of property are invoked and enforced to evict them, if necessary by force. If employees have to work long hours and make little money, it is because of the prevailing rules

of property and contract. The realists believe that private prop-
erty is fine, even good, but they denied that the rules of property
could be identified with liberty. Sometimes those rules disserve
liberty.[20]

There are thousands of brilliant lawyers who can teach constitutional law. But there are relatively few faculty positions at Harvard Law School. Are the rules rigged in academia, where Sunstein
was a tenured professor prior to government service, from competition by others who might want a chance at acquiring the pres-
tige and income that come with such a distinguished position?
Does not tenure, in this case and generally, disserve liberty? Pre-
sumably Sunstein believes he has earned his way. But since his
liberty and property (his job) were not linked, and since the government has the authority to determine what is or is not a property right—and its proper distribution—if Sunstein had been
forced to surrender his post to make room for a more needy or
deserving lawyer who coveted Sunstein's professorship, it would
seem, in Sunstein's formulation of rights, a legitimate function of
government.

Of Sunstein, Ackerman, and West, the late William F. Buckley, Jr., would no doubt repeat his oft-cited quip that "I would
rather be governed by the first two thousand people in the Boston
telephone directory than by the two thousand people on the faculty of Harvard University."[21] As Buckley later elaborated,
"[T]here is a better chance of a repository of the kind of wisdom I
choose to be governed by among average people than among
Ph.D's at Harvard."[22]

Sunstein's manner of thought ignores certain anthropological realities of the human species. In nature, man's progenitors were almost never the fastest, strongest, most agile, deadliest, or toughest creatures in any situation. Moreover, man had little in the way of innate protections against climate extremes and naturally occurring threats to his existence. What differentiated man from the rest of the animal kingdom was, in part, his ability to adapt his behavior to overcome his weaknesses and better master his circumstances. One of the fundamental ways man adapts is to acquire and possess property. It is how he makes his home, finds or grows food, makes clothing, and generally improves his life. Private property is not an artificial construct. It is endemic to human nature and survival.

Sunstein's "realism" is not new. He creates the false choice between anarchy (where there are no laws protecting the individual, private property, and contracts) and tyranny (where the sovereign and the sovereign alone arbitrarily grants fundamental rights, including property rights). Having declared the sovereign paramount to God and nature, and having delinked liberty from property, the individual must rely on the government for his sustenance. Of course, history shows that man will starve and freeze if he relies on the government for his sustenance—and surrender his liberty as well.

The "realists" are an arrogant lot who reject the nation's founding principles. They teach that the Constitution should not be interpreted as the Framers intended—limiting the authority of the federal government through "negative rights," that is, the right not to be abused and coerced by the government; instead, they urge that the Constitution be interpreted as compelling the government to enforce "positive rights," that is, "economic and social justice" or "the Second Bill of Rights." The "realists" plot to transform the civil society through the judiciary—without the consent of the people and without regard to the Constitution. And they are well positioned to do so. There is no denying that the judiciary has assumed the role of final arbiter of the Constitution and that the other branches have acquiesced. As such, the judiciary encourages this kind of pernicious delinquency.

The judiciary today behaves in the manner of an ongoing constitutional convention, unilaterally amending the Constitution almost at will. A majority of Supreme Court justices have, on occasion, even justified the use of foreign law in interpreting the Constitution.[23] The application of customs, traditions, and values that attach to foreign cultures and laws provides no legitimate insight into America's Constitution and diminishes the contemporary role of the state and federal representative branches in writing America's laws and amending (or not) the Constitution. The arbitrary application of foreign law—which provides an activist justice with an infinite smorgasbord of legal options—is a rejection of the predicate for America's governmental system. And it lasts only as long as the next opinion.

In 1850, French philosopher Frédéric Bastiat, writing about the law, summed it up well:

> [W]hen [the law] has exceeded its proper functions, it has not done so merely in some inconsequential and debatable matters. The law has gone further than this; it has acted in direct opposition to its own purpose. The law has been used to destroy its own objective: It has been applied to annihilating the justice that it was supposed to maintain; to limiting and destroying rights

which its real purpose was to respect. The law has placed the collective force at the disposal of the unscrupulous who wish, without risk, to exploit the person, liberty, and property of others. It has converted plunder into a right, in order to protect plunder. And it has converted lawful defense into a crime, in order to punish lawful defense.[24]

5

ON FEDERALISM

IN THE SUMMER OF 1787, when delegates from twelve states met in Philadelphia to rewrite the Articles of Confederation,[1] there were many passionate, detailed debates over the power and scope of the new federal government and the importance of preserving and protecting existing state authority. The Framers knew they needed to replace the Articles, for they did not establish a workable governing system in which the federal and state governments could coexist, each with their own discrete functions and independent—yet in other ways, interdependent—authority. The Framers determined that only in limited areas—including national defense, immigration, issuing currency, raising revenue to operate the national government, foreign relations, resolving conflicts between states, and certain other specific, enumerated circumstances—could the federal government have primary if not exclusive power. In all other respects, the states retained their authority.

The Tenth Amendment generally underscores the division of authority between the federal and state governments:

The powers not delegated to the United States by the Constitution, nor prohibited by it to the States, are reserved to the States respectively, or to the people.[2]

But what was the purpose of this new "federal" system? Along with limiting federal power and separating that power among three competing branches, the federal system would help ensure that the Revolution's principles, as set forth in the Declaration of Independence, and the civil society itself would be safeguarded.

States are governmental entities that reflect the personalities, characteristics, histories, and priorities of the individuals who choose to inhabit them. They have diverse geographies, climates, resources, and populations. No two states are alike. The same can be said of the cities, towns, and hamlets within the states, which number in the tens of thousands and dot the nation's landscape.

States are more likely to better reflect the interests of their citizens than the federal government. Localities are even more likely to better reflect these interests because the decision makers come from the communities they govern—they are directly affected by their own decisions. Moreover, the interaction between the people and their representatives at the state and local levels is easier and more direct. When the federal government acts beyond its constitutional limits, it assaults the purest form of representative government by supplanting representative decision making at the state and local levels. The federal government cannot possibly comprehend the diversity of interests that are affected by its decision making. It cannot adequately weigh the costs and benefits of its decisions on communities. Besides, that is not its purpose. It seeks to dictate rather than represent.

Federalism has other profound benefits. As Associate justice Louis D. Brandeis wrote, "A single courageous state may, if its citizens choose, serve as a laboratory; and try novel social and economic experiments without risk to the rest of the country."[3]

For the Framers, "experimentation," like change, was a matter of prudence. As previously described, change should be informed by the experience, knowledge, and traditions of society, tailored for a specific purpose, and accomplished through a constitutional construct that ensures thoughtful deliberation by the community. Change unconstrained by prudence produces unpredictable consequences, threatening ordered liberty with chaos and ultimately despotism, and placing at risk the very principles the Conservative holds dear.[4] Therefore, while Brandeis was right to acknowledge the import of states in experimenting with public policy, his use of the word *novel* suggests open-ended or unconstrained experimentation.

Whatever kind of experimentation states and local communities may engage in, it is correct to say that they serve as useful examples for adoption, modification, or rejection by other states and localities. In the 1980s, Oregon's welfare reform experiment was so successful that it became a model not only for other states, but also for the federal government.[5] Milwaukee's experiment with school vouchers sparked similar efforts across the country.[6] Experimentation properly understood is a dynamic characteristic of federalism, which exists among, between, and within the various states. That is not to say that all experimentation produces desirable results. When Maryland passed a computer-services tax, its burgeoning technology sector threatened to relocate to neighboring Virginia, which had no such tax.[7] Maryland repealed the tax.[8] But other states learned from Maryland's experience.

Mobility is perhaps the most important aspect of federalism. If the individual concludes he is hopelessly bound by what he considers to be a harmful decision by state or local authorities, he may, in the end, choose to live elsewhere—where the economic, cultural, or social conditions are more to his liking. Indeed, throughout American history, individuals of all races, ages, and income levels have moved from one state to another, either because they are escaping adverse conditions, or simply because they are seeking greener pastures. For example, today large industrial states, which burden their citizens and businesses with high taxes and excessive regulations, are depopulating themselves. Individuals are taking their assets and moving to other parts of the country. Some are moving to states like Florida or Nevada because they have no income tax, or they are relocating their businesses to Alabama because it is a right-to-work state. People move to different states for infinite reasons. Federalism promotes decentralized government, which empowers the individual to choose whether to stay in one place and try to influence the state and local decision making or to take up residence in another state or locality. There is no escaping the reach of the federal government, however, unless one gives up on the country altogether and leaves for other shores.

Federalism also defuses conflict and even promotes harmony. A strong proponent of the death penalty can live in Texas, which has the most active execution chamber, and not care much that

New Jersey just abolished the punishment. Individuals with widely divergent beliefs are able to coexist in the same country because of the diversity and tolerance federalism promotes.

However, one of the most dramatic events undermining state constitutional authority came with the ratification of the Seventeenth Amendment on April 8, 1913.[9] The Seventeenth Amendment changed the method by which senators were chosen, from being selected by the state legislatures—ensuring that the state governments would have a direct and meaningful voice in the operation of the federal government—to direct popular election by the citizens of each state. A rising tide of progressivism and populism resulted in enough states ratifying the amendment that they largely disenfranchised themselves from the federal lawmaking process.

Even with the elimination of their direct representation in the Senate, the states independently possessed considerable authority under the Constitution. Consequently, for the Statist, federalism, like free markets and private property, remained a major obstacle to amassing power. Therefore, he would have to subvert the Constitution to achieve his ends—which he did.

The Constitution's interstate commerce clause had as its purpose the promotion of commerce and trade among the states.[10] However, in 1942 the Supreme Court ruled in *Wickard v. Filburn* that a farmer growing wheat on his own land and for his own use was still subject to federal production limits, even though none of his wheat ever left the state.[11] The Court "reasoned" that by withholding his wheat from commerce, the farmer was affecting interstate commerce, even though there was no commerce, let alone interstate commerce. This meant that private economic activity conducted for the sole purpose of self-consumption and occurring wholly within a state's borders would now be subject to federal regulatory authority under the Agricultural Adjustment Act.[12] *Wickard* swept away 150 years of constitutional jurisprudence, decentralized governmental authority, and private property rights protection. And with it the judiciary seized a role for itself—the manipulation of law to promote a Statist agenda—that continues to this day. Indeed, through a succession of laws and rulings, all three branches—the judicial, the legislative, and the executive— now routinely exercise power well beyond their specific, enumerated authority under the Constitution.

In many respects, the once-powerful states, thirteen of which ratified the Constitution in the first place, have themselves become administrative appendages of the federal government. It is not enough that the federal government exercises authority reserved to the states, but it also blackmails the states to implement its policies by threatening to deny them "their fair share" of federal tax dollars should they object. In fact, so complete is the federal government's authority over the states that it heavily regulates and even monitors them to ensure their compliance with federal dictates. Does anyone believe that the states would have originally ratified the Constitution had they known this would be their fate?

The Statist has also constructed a Fourth Branch of government—an enormous administrative state—which exists to oversee and implement his policies. It is a massive yet amorphous bureaucracy that consists of a workforce of nearly 2 million civilian employees.[13] It administers a budget of over $3 trillion a year.[14] It churns out a mind-numbing number of rules that regulate energy, the environment, business, labor, employment, transportation, housing, agriculture, food, drugs, education, etc. Even the slightest human activity apparently requires its intervention: clothing labels on women's dresses,[15] cosmetics ingredients, and labeling.[16] It even reaches into the bathroom, mandating shower head flow rates and allowable gallons per flush for toilets.[17] It sets flammability standards for beds.[18] There are nearly one thousand federal departments, agencies, and divisions that make laws and enforce them.[19]

The official compilation of rules issued by the federal government, the Federal Register, contained 74,937 pages of regulations in 2006. Tolstoy's *War and Peace*, only 1,400 pages in length, seems as light and airy as a romance novel by comparison. The rules in the Federal Register are written in a dense and confusing style, often confounding the lawyers, accountants, businessmen, and others required to digest them. The estimated cost of simply complying with these regulations was $1.14 trillion.[20] The National Taxpayers Union estimated that in 2006, U.S. businesses and individuals spent 6.65 billion hours struggling to comply with the complexities of the tax code, at a cost of $156.5 billion in lost productivity for businesses alone.[21]

All branches of the federal government, elected and unelected, have consumed more and more of the governing authority of states and localities, leaving them less room to exercise their discretion. In doing so, the federal government is imposing its will directly on communities and citizens in contravention of the Constitution. Consequently, there has been a fundamental breakdown of the federal system.

Having spent decades fighting and losing legal challenges to federal encroachment, states have for the most part accepted the role the Statist has assigned to them. Many governors have become politically expedient on the subject, arguing schizophrenically for federal intervention while defending state preeminence. Even worse, a type of *crony federalism* now exists whereby states lobby the federal government for advantage or relief. It works like this: States convince the federal government to fund projects within their own borders by taxing the citizens of other states. In the name of stimulating the economy, states, counties, cities, and towns have compiled long lists of pork projects they want paid for by the federal taxpayer. They are also asking the federal government to bail them out from their own deficits. For the Statist, the voluntary surrender of state and local authority to the federal government is to be encouraged. Moreover, states with more onerous regulatory standards often urge the federal government to impose those standards on other states to "level the playing field." (Individuals, unions, and businesses also seek federal intervention to supplant state decisions that they do not like.)

The Statist's most successful rhetorical attack on federalism involves slavery and civil rights. He asks, "How can the Conservative defend federalism when state governments were responsible for enslaving and oppressing African-Americans?"

It is a misreading of history to singularly condemn federalism for slavery. While there is no debating or excusing that southern states sanctioned slavery, at times they did so with the help of the federal government. Moreover, there is also no questioning that other states, mostly in the North, instituted policies and laws not only prohibiting slavery within their own borders, but defying efforts by the southern states *and* the federal government to enforce slavery in the South.

For example, prior to the Civil War, and at the behest of the southern states, in 1793 and 1850 the *federal* Fugitive Slave laws were enacted to force recalcitrant northern states to return escaped slaves to their southern owners. Many northern states resisted by passing personal liberty laws, which created legal obstacles to the deportation of slaves back to the South. In the 1842 *Prigg v. Pennsylvania* case,[22] the *federal* Supreme Court ruled these laws unconstitutional, arguing that they sought to preempt federal law, although it added that the northern states were not required to affirmatively assist the southern states that sought the return of escaped slaves. In 1857, the Court ruled in *Dred Scott v. Sandford*[23] that no slaves or descendants of slaves could be U.S. citizens, and that Congress's Missouri Compromise of 1820, which prohibited slavery in much of the new territories, was unconstitutional, for it denied slave owners their personal property rights. As a result, the Court not only denied the slave the ability to escape one state's tyranny for another state's freedom—a direct assault on a critical aspect of federalism, *mobility*—but it actually expanded slavery throughout the country, which helped precipitate the Civil War. Furthermore, not until 1862 did the federal government abolish slavery in the District of Columbia, which was wholly controlled by federal authorities. Therefore, the Statist can be asked, "How can you defend an all-powerful federal government, given its role in promoting slavery?"[24]

Slavery was a contentious issue not only between the states, but also within the states—including in towns and counties in southern states. It was contentious not only between the federal government and the states, but within the federal government— as between Congress and the president, and between the elected branches and the Supreme Court.

The oppression of African-Americans was never compatible with the civil society, although some northern state delegates recognized this fact and sought to abolish slavery at the Constitutional Convention. The southern states would not unite behind such a constitution. It is all the more remarkable, therefore, that certain compromises were reached with the southern state delegates respecting slavery. The constitution they adopted empowered Congress to prohibit the importation of slaves to the United States in twenty years' time,[25] which it did. It reduced the influence southern states would have in the House of Representatives by counting slaves as three-fifths persons for the purpose of apportioning seats.[26] Unfortunately, the southern states did succeed in inserting language requiring the return of slaves who escaped to other states.[27] However, the Constitution did not, as some contend, compel the practice of slavery.

But it must be emphasized that had not the Constitution been adopted, and had the southern states either formed their own nation or simply existed on their own, the institution of slavery would most certainly have survived longer than it did. There would have been no southern state secession because there would have been no union of northern and southern states in the first place. The Constitution's ratification by the southern states would ultimately mark the beginning of the end of slavery—coming to fruition with their defeat in the Civil War and the subsequent adoption by Congress *and* the states of the Thirteenth (formally abolishing slavery), Fourteenth (prohibiting the abridgment of citizens' rights), and Fifteenth (prohibiting race as a bar to voting) Amendments to the Constitution.

A nation founded on the self-evident truth that "all men are created equal, that they are endowed by their Creator with certain unalienable Rights, that among these are Life, Liberty, and the pursuit of Happiness"[28] could not forever tolerate slavery within its midst. And it did not.

For the Conservative, the lesson comes back to man's imperfection. Even good men are capable of bad things. The disgrace of slavery is a disgrace of the human condition—as is all tyranny. Man's institutions, like man himself, are imperfect. They can be used for good or bad, and they have been used for both. Therefore, diffusing authority among many imperfect men—by enumerating federal power, separating power within the federal government, and sharing power with the states—isolates and limits tyranny. Had slavery been affirmed in the Constitution and urged on all states, who knows when and how it would have been abolished.

The Conservative acknowledges that there are occasions when it is difficult to discern the legitimate and preferred demarcation between the different parts and levels of government. But unlike the Statist, he earnestly endeavors to find them. For example, he accepts today, as certain Conservatives may not have yesterday, that the civil rights acts of the 1960s, while excessive in their application in some respects (such as imposing overly broad speech and behavior codes on universities, secular goals on religious institutions, and a wide range of employment and housing restrictions, which ultimately embrace an authoritarian approach that threatens civil liberties),[29] were the proper exercise of federal statutory authority under the Fourteenth Amendment to address intransigent state racism against African-Americans.[30] For the Statist, however, the advantage of a federal government monopoly without effective challenge from a diversity of states or their citizens is obvious: It is a pathway to his precious Utopia where, in the end, all are enslaved in one form or another.

In "Federalist 39," James Madison wrote, in part, "Each State, in ratifying the Constitution, is considered as a sovereign body, independent of all others, and only to be bound by its own voluntary act. In this relation, then, the new Constitution will, if established, be a FEDERAL, and not a NATIONAL constitution."[31]

Of course, today it is more national than federal.

6

ON THE FREE MARKET

THE FREE MARKET IS the most transformative of economic systems. It fosters creativity and inventiveness. It produces new industries, products, and services, as it improves upon existing ones. With millions of individuals freely engaged in an infinite number and variety of transactions each day, it is impossible to even conceive all the changes and plans for changes occurring in our economy at any given time. The free market creates more wealth and opportunities for more people than any other economic model.

But the Conservative believes that the individual is more than a producer and consumer of material goods. He exists within the larger context of the civil society—which provides for an ordered liberty. The Conservative sees in the free market the harmony of interests and rules of cooperation that also underlie the civil society. For example, the free market promotes self-worth, self-sufficiency, shared values, and honest dealings, which enhance the individual, the family, and the community. It discriminates against no race, religion, or gender. The truck driver does not know the skin color of the individuals who produce the diesel fuel for his vehicle; the cook does not know the religion of the dairy farmers who supply milk to his restaurant; and the airline passenger does not know the gender of the factory workers who manufacture the commercial aircraft that transports him—nor do they care.

The free market is an intricate system of voluntary economic, social, and cultural interactions that are motivated by the desires and needs of the individual and the community. The Conservative believes that while the symmetry between the free market and the civil society is imperfect—that is, not all developments resulting from individual interactions contribute to the overall well-being of the civil society—one simply cannot exist without the other.

The key to understanding the free market is *private property*. Private property is the material manifestation of the individual's labor—the material value created from the intellectual and/or physical labor of the individual, which may take the form of income, real property, or intellectual property. Just as life is finite, so, too, is the extent of one's labor. Therefore, taxation of private property, or the regulation of such property so as to reduce its value, can become in effect a form of servitude, particularly if the dispossession results from illegitimate and arbitrary state action. Hence, the Conservative believes that the federal government should raise revenue only to fund those activities that the Constitution authorizes and no others. Otherwise, what are the limits on the Statist's power to tax and regulate the individual's labor and, ultimately, enslave him?

The Marxist class-struggle formulation, which pits the proletariat ("working class") against the bourgeoisie ("wealthy merchant class"), still serves as the principal theoretical and rhetorical justification for the Statist's assault on the free market. But it is an anathema to the free market in that the individual has unto himself the power to make of himself what he chooses. There is no static class structure layered atop the free market. The free market is a mutable, dynamic, and vibrant system of individual interactions that engages all aspects of the human character. For this reason, the Conservative believes the free market is a vital bulwark against statism. And it would appear the Statist agrees, for he is relentless in his assault on it. Indeed, the Statist's rejection of the Constitution's limits on federal power is justified primarily, albeit not exclusively, on material grounds.

In the name of "economic justice" and "equality" the Statist creates the perception of class struggle through a variety of inventions, including the "progressive" income tax. In the *Communist Manifesto*, Karl Marx wrote, "In the most advanced countries the following will be pretty generally applicable: a heavy progressive or graduated income tax."[1]

A recent study by the Organisation for Economic Co-operation and Development found that when measuring household taxes (income taxes and employee Social Security contributions), the United States "has the most progressive tax system and collects the largest share of taxes from the richest 10 percent of the population," placing a heavier tax burden on high-income households than other industrialized nations do.[2] The latest Congressional Budget Office figures show that the top 1 percent of income earners in the United States paid 39 percent of federal income taxes while earning 18 percent of pretax income and the top 5 percent of income earners paid 61 percent of federal income taxes while earning 31 percent of pretax income. Indeed, the top 40 percent of income earners paid 99.4 percent of federal income taxes. The bottom 40 percent of income earners paid no federal income tax and received 3.8 percent from the tax system. And the middle 20 percent of income earners pay only 4.4 percent of federal income taxes.[3]

While the Conservative, like Adam Smith, does not object to wealthier individuals paying more to finance the *legitimate* functions of government, the government has grown well beyond the limits placed on it by the Constitution, particularly since the New Deal. Redistributing wealth is a central objective of the progressive income tax, which Marx would endorse and Smith would reject. For the Statist, there must be a class struggle and it must be a never-ending struggle, for it is perhaps his most valuable weapon in his war against the individual, the free market, and ultimately the civil society. The Statist, therefore, not only opposes efforts to eliminate the progressive income tax, including such alternatives as the FAIR tax (a national sales tax) or the flat tax (a flat-rate income tax), he opposes most any income tax reductions that might weaken the "class structure."

Inasmuch as economic equality is unachievable, even in the most repressive socialist states, it serves the Statist's purpose to contrive a class system in which individuals are grouped by officially sanctioned, arbitrary economic categories. In this way, the Statist stirs up class envy. The free market is, therefore, said to be incapable of serving the public interest, for it produces unjust results, thereby requiring further government intervention. The Statist also attempts to manipulate the intensity of the "class struggle" by routinely redefining terms and categories of wealth—who qualifies as the detested "rich," the righteous "middle class," and the disenfranchised "poor."

But it is the so-called "middle class" that is the object of the Statist's exploitations. He believes if he can win the "working man's" favor, he can win the day. As Marxist community organizer Saul Alinsky explained in *Rules for Radicals*, "Organization for action will now and in the decade ahead center upon America's white middle class. That is where the power is. When more than three-fourths of our people from both the point of view of economics and of their self-identification are middle class, it is obvious that their action or inaction will determine the direction of change. Large parts of the middle class, the 'silent majority,' must be activated; action and articulation are one, as are silence and surrender."[4]

Alinsky continued, ". . . Our rebels have contemptuously rejected the values and way of life of the middle class. They have stigmatized it as materialistic, decadent, bourgeois, degenerate, imperialistic, war-mongering, brutalized, and corrupt. They are right; but we must begin from where we are if we are to build power for change, and the power and the people are in the big middle-class majority."[5] And so it is that for Alinsky, the "middle class" is both celebrated and despised. Alinsky's views were an important influence on President Barack Obama.[6]

A minority of Conservatives agree with Alinsky and Marx only to the extent that they see the future as pandering to the "middle class" or "working class" or "Sam's Club shoppers" or "the suburbs" with appeals of further government intervention aimed at this (or these) loosely defined grouping(s) of citizens. But who populates this "middle class"? Is the twenty-five-year-old female paralegal who graduated from college, works at a large law firm, earns $85,000 a year, is unmarried and without children, lives in an apartment in Manhattan, and rarely attends church in the same "middle class" as the fifty-seven-year-old male auto mechanic who did not graduate from high school, works at Pep Boys, earns $55,000 a year, lives in a row home in northeast Philadelphia, is married with four children, and attends church every Sunday? For the Conservative, this manner of thinking has the potential to evolve into a politically dangerous myopia that substitutes the hard work of advancing conservative principles and preserving the civil society with a political strategy that has ephemeral usefulness yet suggests universal acceptance of a static class structure that is foreign to the free market and civil society. This manner of thinking also places artificial constraints on conservatism's attractiveness by focusing too much on the wrong thing.

For the Conservative, the challenge is to deconstruct the Statist class argument and inspire the individual to appreciate the miracle of the free market and enthusiastically engage in it. He should emphasize that the free market is the only economic system that produces on a sustainable basis, and for the overwhelming majority of Americans, an abundance of food, housing, energy, and medicine—the staples of human survival; it creates an astonishing array of consumer goods that add comfort, value, and security to the qualify of life; and the free market recognizes that it is in man's DNA to take risks, to innovate, to achieve, to compete, and to acquire—to not only survive but also improve his circumstance.

Furthermore, the Conservative should appeal to man's nature.

He should emphasize that the individual knows better how to make and spend that which he has earned from his own labor and provide for his family than do large bureaucracies populated by strangers who see classes of people rather than individual human beings. As Founder James Wilson observed, "By exclusive property, the productions of the earth and the means of subsistence are secured and preserved, as well as multiplied. What belongs to no one is wasted by every one. What belongs to one man in particular is the object of his economy and care."[7]

The Statist seeks to impose on individuals a governmental and economic structure that is contrary to human nature. He attempts to control the individual by subverting his spirit and punishing his natural impulses. For example, the parent teaches the child that stealing is wrong. Faith also teaches it is immoral: "Thou shalt not steal." Laws, in turn, make it a crime to steal. One can only imagine the complete breakdown of the civil society that would result if stealing were an acceptable practice. For the Statist, however, thievery by government is a virtue in that it is said to be compelled for the "public good" or in the "public interest."

Who then decides what is good for the public or in the public interest? The Constitution provides the parameters within which the federal government has authority to act. How does violating those parameters, which are intended to secure individual liberty (including private property rights) against the tyranny of an all-too-powerful government, serve the public interest?

Moreover, from where does the Statist acquire his clairvoyance in determining what is good for the public? From his ideology. The Statist is constantly manipulating public sentiment in a steady effort to disestablish the free market, as he pushes the nation down tyranny's road. He has built an enormous maze of government agencies and programs, which grow inexorably from year to year, and which intervene in and interfere with the free market. And when the Statist's central planners create economic perversions that are seriously detrimental to the public, he blames the free market and insists on seizing additional authority to correct the failures created at his own direction.

Consider the four basic events that led to the housing bust of 2008, which spread to the financial markets and beyond:

EVENT 1: In 1977, Congress passed the Community Reinvestment Act (CRA) to address alleged discrimination by banks in making loans to poor people and minorities in the inner cities (redlining). The act provided that banks have "an affirmative obligation" to meet the credit needs of the communities in which they are chartered.[8] In 1989, Congress amended the Home Mortgage Disclosure Act requiring banks to collect racial data on mortgage applications.[9] University of Texas economics professor Stan Liebowitz has written that "minority mortgage applications were rejected more frequently than other applications, but the overwhelming reason wasn't racial discrimination, but simply that minorities tend to have weaker finances."[10] Liebowitz also condemns a 1992 study conducted by the Boston Federal Reserve Bank that alleged systemic discrimination. "That study was tremendously flawed. A colleague and I . . . showed that the data it had used contained thousands of egregious typos, such as loans with negative interest rates. Our study found no evidence of discrimination."[11] However, the study became the standard on which government policy was based.

In 1995, the Clinton administration's Treasury Department issued regulations tracking loans by neighborhoods, income groups, and races to rate the performance of banks. The ratings were used by regulators to determine whether the government would approve bank mergers, acquisitions, and new branches.[12] The regulations also encouraged statist-aligned groups, such as the Association of Community Organizations for Reform Now (ACORN) and the Neighborhood Assistance Corporation of America, to file petitions with regulators, or threaten to, to slow or even prevent banks from conducting their business by challenging the extent to which banks were issuing these loans. With such powerful leverage over banks, some groups were able, in effect, to legally extort banks to make huge pools of money available to the groups, money they in turn used to make loans. The banks and community groups issued loans to low-income individuals who often had bad credit or insufficient income. And these loans, which became known as "subprime" loans, made available 100 percent financing, did not always require the use of credit scores, and were even made without documenting income.[13] Therefore, the government insisted that banks, particularly those that wanted to expand, abandon traditional underwriting standards. One estimate puts the figure of CRA-eligible loans at $4.5 trillion.[14]

EVENT 2: In 1992, the Department of Housing and Urban Development pressured two government-chartered corporations—known as Freddie Mac and Fannie Mae—to purchase (or "securitize") large bundles of these loans for the conflicting purposes of diversifying the risk and making even more money available to banks to make further risky loans. Congress also passed the Federal Housing Enterprises Financial Safety and Soundness Act, eventually mandating that these companies buy 45 percent of all loans from people of low and moderate incomes.[15] Consequently, a secondary market was created for these loans. And in 1995, the Treasury Department established the Community Development Financial Institutions Fund, which provided banks with tax dollars to encourage even more risky loans.

For the Statist, however, this still was not enough. Top congressional Democrats, including Representative Barney Frank (Massachusetts), Senator Christopher Dodd (Connecticut), and Senator Charles Schumer (New York), among others, repeatedly ignored warnings of pending disaster, insisting that they were overstated, and opposed efforts to force Freddie Mac and Fannie Mae to comply with usual business and oversight practices.[16] And the top executives of these corporations, most of whom had worked in or with Democratic administrations, resisted reform while they were actively cooking the books in order to award themselves tens of millions of dollars in bonuses.[17]

EVENT 3: A by-product of this government intervention and social engineering was a financial instrument called the "derivative," which turned the subprime mortgage market into a ticking time bomb that would magnify the housing bust by orders of magnitude. A derivative is a contract where one party sells the risk associated with the mortgage to another party in exchange for payments to that company based on the value of the mortgage. In some cases, investors who did not even make the loans would bet on whether the loans would be subject to default. Although imprecise, perhaps derivatives in this context can best be understood as a form of insurance. Derivatives allowed commercial and investment banks, individual companies, and private investors to further spread—and ultimately multiply—the risk associated with their mortgages. Certain financial and insurance institutions invested heavily in derivatives, such as American International Group (AIG).[18]

EVENT 4: The Federal Reserve Board's role in the housing boom-and-bust cannot be overstated. The Pacific Research Institute's Robert P. Murphy explains that "[the Federal Reserve] slashed interest rates repeatedly starting in January 2001, from 6.5 percent until they reached a low in June 2003 of 1.0 percent. (In nominal terms, this was the lowest the target rate had been in the entire data series maintained by the St. Louis Federal Reserve, going back to 1982). . . . When the easy-money policy became too inflationary for comfort, the Fed (under [Alan] Greenspan and then new Chairman Ben Bernanke at the end) began a steady process of raising interest rates back up, from 1.0 percent in June 2004 to 5.25 percent in June 2006. . . ."[19] Therefore, when the Federal Reserve abandoned its role as steward of the monetary system and used interest rates to artificially and inappropriately manipulate the housing market, it interfered with normal market conditions and contributed to destabilizing the economy.

In 2008 and 2009, the federal government spent tax dollars at a frenzied pace to try to rescue the financial markets from its own mismanagement. Troubled Asset Relief Program (TARP) outlays could reach $1 trillion or 7 percent of the nation's gross domestic product. TARP was originally enacted so the government could buy risky or nonperforming loans from financial institutions. But the mission changed within weeks—the government began using the funds to buy equity positions in financial institutions, presumably to inject cash directly into these entities. An oversight panel concluded that $350 billion of the TARP funds cannot be adequately accounted for.[20]

The Federal Reserve also provided assistance of $30 billion for Bear Stearns, $150 billion for AIG, $200 billion for Fannie Mae and Freddie Mac, $20 billion for Citigroup, $245 billion for the commercial paper market, and $540 billion for the money markets.[21] It is poised to lend over *$7 trillion* to financial institutions, or over half the size of the entire American economy in 2007.[22]

According to Bianco Research president James Bianco, the federal bailout far exceeds nine of the costliest events in American history combined:

Event	Cost	Inflation-Adjusted Cost
Marshall Plan	$12.7 billion	$115.3 billion
Louisiana Purchase	$15 million	$217 billion
Race to the Moon	$36.4 billion	$237 billion
S&L Crisis	$153 billion	$236 billion
Korean War	$54 billion	$454 billion
The New Deal	$32 billion (est.)	$500 billion (est.)
Invasion of Iraq	$551 billion	$597 billion
Vietnam War	$111 billion	$698 billion
NASA	$416 billion	$851.2 billion
TOTAL		Over $3.9 trillion.[23]

The entire cost of World War II to the United States was $288 billion, or $3.6 trillion when adjusted for inflation.[24]

Congress also passed, and President George W. Bush signed, fiscal spending bills to try to alleviate the economy's ills, such as the $152 billion Economic Stimulus Act of 2008[25] and the $300 billion Housing and Economic Recovery Act of 2008.[26] Congress and President Barack Obama are upping the ante by hundreds of billions more or so with the so-called American Recovery and Reinvestment Plan of 2009.[27]

The *Wall Street Journal* reports that when stimulus and bailout spending is combined, "the federal spending share of GDP will climb to 27.5%." Put another way, more than $1 of every $4 produced by the economy will be consumed or controlled by the federal government. The *Journal* also notes that "all of this is fast pushing the U.S. to European spending levels, and that's before Obama's new health-care entitlements."[28]

The crisis created in the financial markets is of the Statist's making. But he learns nothing from the destruction he unleashes, for he is not motivated by virtue and he does not act with prudence. Instead, his framework is ideological. As President Obama's chief of staff, Rahm Emanuel, openly admitted, "Rule one: Never allow a crisis to go to waste. They are opportunities to do big things."[29] By wrestling decision making from the free market, the Statist is able to exercise enormous control over the individual and society generally.

The oil industry is a favorite target of the Statist, since fuel runs the engine of America's vast economy. The Statist knows that the consumer is particularly sensitive to increases in gasoline prices because of his frequent visits to the gas station. The Statist tells him that these increases are due to "greed," "profiteering," and "price gouging" by the oil companies. Of course, oil is a commodity in worldwide demand, with use in China and India, the earth's most populous nations, growing rapidly. Approximately 70 percent of the price of a gallon of gasoline is the cost of crude oil.[30] Therefore, supply and demand on the world market directly influence availability and pricing in the United States.

But apart from the world market, the Statist will never and must never concede that *he* is sabotaging the provision of affordable, reliable, domestic supplies of energy by significantly and purposefully driving up costs to the oil companies in addition to worldwide supply and price influences. The Statist's heavy hand has gripped the oil industry for more than one hundred years. The oil industry is hardly free to operate as efficiently as it could or to be as responsive to consumer demands as it would like. It has become, in essence, a quasi-state-run enterprise, because it cannot drill, transport, refine, and store fuel without receiving government permission, complying with government regulations, and paying taxes at every level of production.

When the Statist prevents the oil companies from drilling new wells in places such as Alaska, the Great Lakes, and most coastal areas, he is driving down the supply of domestic crude oil and gasoline. How can a nation cut itself off from most of its energy resources and hope to prosper or, in the long run, even survive?

Moreover, America's refining capacity has not changed much over the last thirty years. As *Investor's Business Daily* reported in March 2008, no new refinery has been built in the United States since 1983. "In 1982, the U.S. economy was served by 301 refineries. By 2007, the number had dwindled to 149. Productivity has kept output steady over the years at 17 million barrels a day. But the U.S. economy has grown by 125%."[31]

The Statist has created a myriad of regulations that dictate a long list of gasoline "blends" as well as seasonal and regional variants that create costly complexities and inefficiencies in the domestic production of usable fuel products. Expanding existing refineries or building new plants must meet newer and more onerous regulations than those applicable to older refineries.[32] These are all hidden, government-imposed surcharges that are magnified throughout the economy and, in the end, are borne by the consumer.

The Statist deflects public scorn for the consequences of his own central planning by blaming the very industry he is sabotaging for supply dislocations and price hikes. He conducts aggressive public relations campaigns that consist of congressional show trials where oil executives are forced to appear before committees and television cameras and defend their business activities in testimony given under the penalty of perjury—as if they may have committed some crime. To underscore this perception, the Statist regularly calls for federal investigations of the oil industry, alleging "collusion," "monopolistic practices," or other illegal conspiracies. Invariably, the investigations clear rather than indict these businesses.

And what of those oil industry profits? Much reporting on oil company revenues, with headlines shouting "oil companies made record profits," is sophomoric and misleading. Rather than serving as watchdogs of the government, too many in the media give voice to the most demagogic statists. In 2007, the oil companies earned between eight and nine cents for every dollar of gasoline sales.[33]

Again, *Investor's Business Daily* recently summed up the oil industry profit situation this way:

From 1977 to 2004, according to Tax Foundation data, U.S. oil companies cleared $630 billion after taxes while paying $518 billion in federal and state corporate taxes at an average rate of 45%. Over the same period, an additional $1.34 trillion in excise fuel taxes was collected from consumers by the oil companies and turned over to various governments.[34]

Government, not the oil industry, is the biggest "profiteer" from oil. And it uses the tax revenue to expand its own authority at the expense of the individual, as it does with an endless number of other industries—including electric power, coal, lumber, pharmaceuticals, automobiles, aircraft, and agriculture. The Statist's intrusion in the free market is boundless.

However, it should be emphasized that the Conservative is not a corporatist—that is, he is not a special pleader for oil companies or any other corporations. He defends free markets because he defends the civil society and the Constitution's limitations on federal authority against the tyranny that threatens them. Therefore, the Conservative also opposes *crony capitalism*, where the Statist uses the power of government—often at the behest of a given industry or corporation—to subsidize one favored enterprise at the expense of another. The Statist's purpose, as always, is to extend his own reach.

For example, ethanol has been around since the 1800s. If it were a viable alternative or additive to gasoline, which supposedly would reduce oil use, gasoline prices, and automobile emissions, the free market would have responded positively. But the consumer and the producer were not all that interested. Of course, that did not dissuade the Statist. For years, large agricultural corporations and environmental groups have lobbied the federal government to promote ethanol production and use. Having already severely damaged the supply of domestic oil, the Statist responded to the lobbying efforts by using tax dollars to heavily subsidize ethanol production, imposing tariffs on the importation of ethanol, forcing the automobile industry to build more ethanol-friendly vehicles, and setting mandates on domestic ethanol production and use levels—15 percent of American cars are to run on ethanol by 2017.[35]

As ethanol and other biofuels require corn, sugarcane, and additional crops to produce blends of gasoline, these essential crops are diverted from food production to energy production. And as demand for corn and sugarcane increases, more farmers around the world respond by converting their fields from rice, wheat, and soy to the more profitable crops used in biofuels. Government policy played a significant role in driving up demand and prices not only for fuel but food, contributing mightily to severe food shortages and even famine in the Third World.

As demand for corn increased in the United States, and since corn in one form or another is fed to most livestock, the price of beef, fowl, and dairy products went up as well. A ripple effect occurs across the economic and global landscape.

And what of the supposed environmental benefits of ethanol? The Associated Press reported:

Ethanol is much less efficient [than gasoline], especially when it is made from corn. Just growing corn requires expending energy—plowing, planting, fertilizing and harvesting all require machinery that burns fossil fuel. Modern agriculture relies on large amounts of fertilizer and pesticides, both of which are produced by methods that consume fossil fuels. Then there's the cost of transporting the corn to an ethanol plant, where the fermentation and distillation processes consume yet more energy. Finally, there's the cost of transporting the fuel to filling stations. And because ethanol is more corrosive than gasoline, it can't be pumped through relatively efficient pipelines, but must be transported by rail or tanker truck. In the end, even the most generous analysts estimate that it takes the energy equivalent of three gallons of gasoline to make four gallons of the stuff. . . . [36]

The Statist, therefore, created instability and unpredictability across various industries with detrimental consequences, intended and unintended, across the globe. Yet he will not take a step back.

There are times when the Statist interferes with the free market to try to stave off what the late economist Joseph Schumpeter, among others, described as *creative destruction*. As he explained,

Capitalism . . . is by nature a form or method of economic change and not only never is but never can be stationary. . . . The fundamental impulse that sets and keeps the capitalist engine in motion comes from the new consumers, goods, the new methods of production or transportation, the new markets, the new forms of industrial organization that enterprise creates . . . [T]he history of the productive apparatus of a typical farm, from the beginnings of the rationalization of crop rotation, plowing and fattening to the mechanized thing of today—linking up with elevators and railroads—is a history of revolutions. So is the history of the productive apparatus of the iron and steel industry from the charcoal furnace to our own type of furnace, of the history of the apparatus of power production from the overshot water wheel to the modern power plant, or the history of transportation from the mail coach to the airplane. The opening up of new markets, foreign or domestic, and the organizational development from the craft shop and the factory to such concerns as U.S. Steel illustrate the same process of industrial mutation . . . that incessantly revolutionizes the economic structure from within, incessantly destroying the old one, incessantly creating a new one. This process of Creative Destruction is the essential fact about capitalism. It is what capitalism consists in and what every capitalist concern has got to live in. . . . [37]

Today, the American automobile industry, once the envy of the world, faces the prospect of creative destruction. Henry Ford perfected the use of the assembly line in the mass production of the Model T. He changed the face of America and the world. Over time, however, it became another favorite target of the Statist. The Wagner Act of 1935 granted monopoly power to unions to bargain for certain employees and call strikes, thereby enabling them to charge monopoly rates for their labor. Beginning in its heyday in the 1950s and 1960s, the United Auto Workers (UAW) used its negotiating muscle to extract progressively onerous and untenable salary and benefit concessions from American automobile manufacturers under the threat of debilitating strikes. Consequently, the American automakers are saddled with costs that make it extremely difficult to compete with nonunion, foreign manufacturers in the United States and overseas.

The Heritage Foundation found that UAW workers at U.S.

factories cost more than $70 per hour compared with a cost per hour for nonunion Japanese autoworkers in the United States of $42 to $48 per hour. With combined wages and benefits, the UAW worker costs nearly $130,000 per year, while the nonunion worker costs about $80,000 a year. Under UAW contracts, workers are not laid off. They are paid nearly full wages not to work for a period of years. And workers can retire after thirty years on the job, no matter their age, and receive pension and health benefits for the rest of their lives.[38]

In addition to wages and benefits, the UAW's inefficient work rules make it difficult for American automakers to adapt to economic conditions and consumer demand.[39] Ford's contract with the UAW is 2,215 pages long.[40] Of course, management entered into a series of contracts over the years agreeing to these arrangements. However, the power of the UAW under the Wagner Act ultimately made management's resistance futile.

In 2007, Congress passed new Corporate Average Fuel Economy (CAFE) standards, costing the U.S. auto industry an additional $110 billion in research, manufacturing, production, and related compliance costs.[41] A high-level automobile industry source expects that by the time the new standards are fully implemented, the consumer will pay an additional $5,000–$6,000 per vehicle. And the average 2007 model car is already carrying at least $2,000 in additional "up front" costs for recently mandated safety equipment.[42] Add to this the wild swings in fuel costs resulting, in large part, from the government's interference in the energy market—making it difficult to predict consumer demand in the out years—by 2008, General Motors and Chrysler were essentially broke, and Ford was on the brink.

It cannot be said that the American automobile industry's critical condition is a result of an unfettered free market. The Statist has played a central role in its undoing and has made a mess of the once vibrant industry. However, does this justify the taxpayer bailing out the industry and the UAW with tens of billions of dollars in subsidies? The answer is no.

The current model of manufacturing American automobiles and organizing employees is unsustainable. So, too, is the government's unrelenting interference in the auto industry's management, labor relations, vehicle designs, etc. The Big Three must seek relief in bankruptcy, which will allow them to newly organize their businesses, including eliminating some of their more onerous operational and labor restrictions, and to become more responsive to modern conditions. The Statist, however, remains an implacable problem. He is not subject to creative destruction. Rather, he hangs over the market as a dark cloud. Even as he dangles billions of dollars in bailout money before the industry, the Statist insists on further advancing the destructive agendas of his environmental and labor constituencies, whose support he needs to continue in power. As the *Wall Street Journal* reported, "When is $25 billion in taxpayer cash insufficient to bail out Detroit's auto makers? Answer: When the money is a tool of Congressional industrial policy to turn GM, Ford and Chrysler into agents of the Sierra Club and other green lobbies."[43] Another crisis, another opportunity.

And Big Labor is to be rewarded, too—having poured tens of millions of dollars in campaign cash into the latest Democratic campaigns and seen its numbers dwindle from about one-third of the workforce in the 1950s to 12 percent today.[44] Not satisfied with its part in breaking the American automobile industry (not to mention the airline and steel industries), the Statist proposes making it easier to unionize other businesses whose workers have chosen not to join their ranks. A bill with the laughable title "The Employee Free Choice Act" would replace secret-ballot elections held on a given day and supervised by the National Labor Relations Board with a process whereby employees would be pressured by union organizers to sign undated cards over a period of perhaps months. Gone will be the secret ballot. Even the 1972 Democratic presidential candidate, George McGovern, has denounced this effort: "To fail to ensure the right to vote free of intimidation and coercion from all sides would be a betrayal of what we have always championed. . . ."[45] President Obama strongly supports the bill.

For the Statist, creative destruction too often means the diminution of his own authority and opportunities to expand it. There are also those, however, with no similar agenda but who cringe nonetheless at the notion, for they are attentive only to the moment. As the Cato Institute's Will Wilkinson observes,

> The impulse to freeze the system, to try to tape all the cracks and staple all the cleavages, to ensure that nobody has to explain to their kid why Christmas this year is going to be a lousy Christmas, that is one of our greatest dangers. Our sympathy, untutored by a grasp of the larger scheme, can perversely make itself ever more necessary. When we feel compelled to act on our uncoached fellow-feeling, next year's Christmas is likely to turn a bit worse for everybody. And then somebody has to explain to the kids that they can't find a job at all. Businesses that

would get started don't get started, wealth that would be created isn't. And in just a few decades, the prevailing standard of living is much, much lower than it could have been had our sympathy been more far-seeing. There is no justice, and great harm, in diminishing the whole array of future opportunity to save a few people now from a regrettable fate.[46]

Comprehend a future without creative destruction. It is bleak, backwards, and destitute, like most authoritarian societies. Yet the Statist has persuaded some erstwhile conservatives of its de-merits. Typically the argument is formulated around protecting America's industrial base. The question is asked: How can Amer-ica allow its industries to fail and outsource its vital needs to other countries? From where will we get our steel? How will we build our tanks? This is a circular argument. The Conserva-tive urges an economic environment stripped of debilitating reg-ulations and taxes that hinder the performance and competition of American industry. He believes American industry is more than capable of competing against foreign industries and, in most cases, does so. However, where industries are subjected to the Statist's heavy hand rather than the free market's invisible hand, they are obstructed and burdened in ways that are counter-intuitive and self-defeating.[47] Ultimately, it is an unworkable for-mula, as the rest of the world is not obliged to adhere to it but rather will look for ways to exploit it. The Statist, therefore, is destructive of the very ends and the very people he professes to represent.

The Statist frequently attempts to relieve himself of responsi-bility for his own deeds by invoking the mantra of "outsourcing"—

that is, the hiring of workers and businesses abroad to undertake tasks that might conceivably be performed in the United States. In 2004, Democratic Presidential candidate John Kerry railed against "Benedict Arnold CEOs" who send American jobs overseas.[48] In 2008, Obama asserted that "we have to stop providing tax breaks for companies that are shipping jobs overseas and give those tax breaks to companies that are investing here in the United States of America."[49] The Statist urges the view that millions of jobs are lost to such practices and complains about every call center that opens in India. He creates the impression that there are no benefits to American society to hiring foreign workers and is not above instigating ethnic animosity. However, the facts do not support the hyperbole.

Jacob Funk Kirkegaard, a research associate at the Peterson Institute for International Economics, studied the official statistics for "mass layoffs" (fifty or more people) in the United States. He found about 1 million people out of a workforce of roughly 150 million were part of a mass layoff in 2004 and 2005. Only a small percentage of these layoffs were due to the exportation of jobs. Kirkegaard wrote, "the combined employment effects of offshoring and offshore outsourcing represent just 4 percent of all separations from mass layoffs in the United States in 2004–05."[50]

And what of the "giant sucking sound" of jobs moving to, say, Mexico as a result of the North American Free Trade Agreement (NAFTA)—which essentially eliminated numerous trade barriers among Mexico, Canada, and the United States? Those job losses would have shown up in American unemployment statistics. Yet once NAFTA took effect in 1994, unemployment generally declined.[51] In 2007, before the recent economic downturn, the average unemployment rate was 4.7 percent, below the prevailing rates in the 1970s, 1980s, and 1990s.[52]

The Statist ignores the benefits of free trade, because it undermines his agenda. When a computer company lowers costs by opening a call center in India, the price of the computer goes down, benefiting American consumers. Money is then freed up in the United States to spend more productively. As Indians become wealthier, they buy more goods and services from the United States. In the past several years, some of the fastest growth in American goods and services exports has been to India.[53]

And what of the benefits of foreign investment pouring into the United States—or "insourcing"? According to the Commerce Department, foreign investment created 447,000 new jobs in the United States between 2003 and 2007.[54] In 2007, 5.3 million Americans were employed by U.S. subsidiaries of foreign companies. These companies maintained a payroll of $364.2 billion for American workers.[55]

Still, the mentality of which Wilkinson writes—resistance against the free market's creative nature—has its origin in myths perpetuated about the Great Depression and the New Deal, which have fostered a tolerance, if not demand, for government intervention in a supposedly flawed and unrestrained market system.

The seeds for the Great Depression were actually sown before the stock market crash of 1929. In 1928, during a recession and struggling housing market, the Federal Reserve Board severely cut the money supply. The discount rate to banks was increased four times, from 3.5 percent to 6 percent from January 1928 to August

1929. (In fact, the money supply shrank 30 percent over the next three years.) By slashing the money supply and cutting off lines of available credit, the economy contracted. At the same time, Congress was debating the passage of the Smoot-Hawley Tariff Act, which was the most draconian protectionist bill in American history. Investors reacted. The stock market became unstable and, over a three-day period in October 1929, it crashed.[56]

President Herbert Hoover, who today is widely and wrongly considered a hands-off, free-market disciple, signed the Smoot-Hawley Tariff into law in June 1930. This came on top of the Fordney-McCumber Tariff of 1922, which had already dealt a terrible blow to the agricultural economy. These tariffs slammed the door on the importation of foreign produce and goods, igniting an international trade war that blocked the exportation of domestic produce and goods to foreign markets. In 1930 and 1931, federal spending soared, with hundreds of millions of dollars in subsidies paid to farmers. Congress established the Reconstruction Finance Corporation, which distributed hundreds of millions of dollars to businesses. In 1932, Hoover signed the Revenue Act—the largest tax increase in peacetime history—doubling the income tax rate. The top bracket jumped from 24 percent to 63 percent.[57] Efforts by Hoover, Congress, and the Federal Reserve to limit the effects of a recession turned into a monumental disaster.

In 1932, Franklin Roosevelt ran against Hoover on a platform of cutting taxes, cutting subsidies, cutting government, and balancing the budget. Upon taking office, however, Roosevelt radically changed direction. As Roosevelt advisor Rexford Guy Tugwell would later explain, "We didn't admit it at the time, but practically the whole New Deal was extrapolated from programs that Hoover started."[58]

Lawrence W. Reed of the Mackinac Center for Public Policy notes that during the course of his presidency, Roosevelt raised the top income tax rate to 79 percent and then 90 percent. He instituted the National Industrial Recovery Act (NIRA) in June 1933, which forced manufacturing industries into government-mandated cartels and empowered a massive federal bureaucracy to dictate production and pricing standards covering two million employers and 22 million workers. Although the Supreme Court eventually ruled the act unconstitutional, the damage had been done. Industrial production dropped 25 percent in the six months after the law had passed. Roosevelt established the Civil Works Administration and later the Works Progress Administration, which have been hailed as putting the unemployed to work on constructing roads, bridges, and buildings. But they were rife with waste and corruption.[59] And as Amity Shlaes, author of *The Forgotten Man: A New History of the Great Depression*, explains, "Evidence from that period suggests that government was crowding out the private sector. The Tennessee Valley Authority, for example, dealt mortal blows to a private employer that wanted to electrify the South. . . . For every state-relief job created, about half a private-sector job was lost."[60] They did nothing to improve the systemic unemployment problem in the country. Indeed, Roosevelt oversaw the implementation of hundreds of laws, regulations, policies, and spending programs, and the creation of numerous agencies to enforce them. And it is clear that in doing so, he prolonged the economic despair of tens of millions of Americans by exacerbating the Great Depression.

Reed recounts that Roosevelt's treasury secretary, Henry Morgenthau, Jr., wrote in his private diary that "we have tried spending money. We are spending more than we have ever spent before and it does not work. . . . We have never made good on our promises. . . . I say after eight years of this Administration we have just as much unemployment as when we started . . . and an enormous debt to boot!"[61] At no time during the eight years of the Great Depression under Roosevelt did the unemployment figure drop below 14 percent. And the unemployment statistics (by percentage) underscore Morgenthau's lament:

1930—8.9
1931—15.9
1932—23.6
1933—24.9
1934—21.7
1935—20.1
1936—17.0
1937—14.3
1938—19.0
1939—17.2
1940—14.6
1941—9.9
1942—4.7[62]

According to an extensive 2004 study by UCLA economists Harold L. Cole and Lee E. Ohanian, Roosevelt's "ill-conceived stimulus policies" extended the Depression by seven years. Ohanian relates that "high wages and high prices in an economic slump run contrary to everything we know about market forces in economic downturns. As we've seen in the past several years, salaries and prices fall when unemployment is high. By artificially inflating both, the New Deal policies short-circuited the market's self-correcting forces."[63] The economists point out that the NIRA exempted more than five hundred industries—accounting for about 80 percent of private, nonagricultural employment—from antitrust prosecution as an incentive to entering into collective bargaining agreements with unions. This drove up prices and wages. They conclude that the Depression would have ended in 1936 instead of 1943. Cole explains, "The fact that the Depression dragged on for years convinced generations of economists and policy-makers that capitalism could not be trusted to recover from depressions and that significant government intervention was required to achieve good outcomes. Ironically, our work shows that the recovery would have been very rapid had the government not intervened."[64]

The fact is that the New Deal was, overall, a dismal failure. Yet today it serves as the Statist's prototype for governance. In 2009, President Obama and Congress spent hundreds of billions of dollars on a new so-called stimulus bill. But it, like the New Deal, will only retard economic growth, create market dislocations, and add to the government's existing massive debt.

The reason stimulus plans of this sort do not work is a fundamental reality of governance: The government does not add value to the economy. It removes value from the economy by imposing taxes on one citizen and providing cash to another. Or it borrows money that would otherwise be used by investors and redistributes it elsewhere. Or it prints more money and threatens the value of the dollar. Nothing is stimulated. Spending power is not increased. Moreover, politicians and bureaucrats are substituting their uninformed, largely political decisions for those of the marketplace. Their past miscalculations demonstrate that they do not and cannot possess the information, knowledge, means, and discipline to manage the economy.

Of course, the best way to stimulate the economy would be for the federal government to slash capital gains taxes, corporate income taxes, and individual income tax rates, thereby increasing liquidity available to *individuals and businesses* to make decisions about their own economic circumstances. Since most people do not hide their cash in cigar boxes, the additional money would either be spent or invested. The more favorable investment environment would also attract the flow of foreign investment into American markets from countries that tax their citizens and businesses at higher rates. Furthermore, the stock market would react favorably to market-oriented spending and savings and it would benefit directly from increased equity purchases resulting from increased investor confidence.

Along these lines, in 1981, when the economy was reeling from double-digit interest, unemployment, and inflation rates, President Ronald Reagan championed the passage of the Economic Recovery Tax Act (the Kemp-Roth bill). It cut individual federal income tax brackets by 25 percent, phased over three years, and indexed the rates against inflation to prevent creeping bracket increases in future years. The act also instituted the Accelerated Cost Recovery System and a 10 percent Investment Tax Credit, which led to a substantial increase in capital formation. The goal was to create incentives by removing significant government barriers to investment, productivity, and growth. The result: Inflation dropped from 13.5 percent in 1980 to 4.1 percent in 1988. Interest rates dropped from 18 percent on a thirty-year fixed mortgage in 1981 to 8 percent in 1987; and unemployment dropped from a peak near 10 percent in the recession of 1981–82 to 5.5 percent in 1989, once the full force of the tax cuts kicked in.[65] The Reagan economic program, based largely on free market principles, spurred economic prosperity that created, over the next twenty-five years, forty-three million jobs and $30 trillion in wealth.[66]

But the Statist is committed to a different course. He is unmoved by reason, evidence, and history. The danger to the individual and the civil society from his constant assault on liberty and private property cannot be emphasized enough. The late economist Friedrich Hayek, in his classic book *The Road to Serfdom*, wrote:

> *Nobody saw more clearly than the great political thinker de Tocqueville that democracy stands in an irreconcilable conflict with socialism: "Democracy extends the sphere of individual freedom," he said. "Democracy attaches all possible value to each man," he said in 1848, "while socialism makes each man a mere agent, a mere number. Democracy and socialism have nothing in common but one word: equality. But notice the difference: while democracy seeks equality in liberty, socialism seeks equality in restraint and servitude."*
>
> *To allay these suspicions and to harness to its cart the strongest of all political motives—the craving for freedom—socialists began increasingly to make use of the promise of a "new free-*

dom." Socialism was to bring "economic freedom," without which political freedom was "not worth having."

To make this argument sound plausible, the word "freedom" was subjected to a subtle change in meaning. The word had formerly meant freedom from coercion, from the arbitrary power of other men. Now it was made to mean freedom from necessity, release from the compulsion of the circumstances which inevitably limit the range of choice of all of us. Freedom in this sense is, of course, merely another name for power or wealth. The demand for the new freedom was thus only another name for the old demand for a redistribution of wealth.[67]

In the free market, a man born into wealth or who has otherwise acquired great riches can lose his fortune depending on how he chooses to behave. Conversely, a man born into poverty or who has lost wealth once obtained can acquire a fortune, depending, again, on how he chooses to behave. When the individual or even a large business makes a wrong decision, its impact is limited and more easily absorbed by the free market. However, when the Statist makes a wrong decision, its impact is far-reaching, for he uses the power of government to impose his decision on as many individuals and businesses as possible, which distorts the free market itself.

The free market can never be completely suppressed even in the most repressive regimes. But in a soft tyranny, where government intervention is pervasive but not absolute, the individual and society still pay a heavy price from the government's diversion of resources, which otherwise might have been used to develop new technologies, products, medicines, jobs, etc., that better serve both the individual and society. Economists call this *lost opportunity costs*. It is difficult if not impossible to quantify that which might have been had the government not intervened, because it is impossible to identify the untold number of individuals who would have been party to an untold number of interactions and transactions had they been free to choose their own course. Morever, lost opportunity costs are often concealed from the individual, since the government's intrusion in the free market is usually incremental and often indirect.

Furthermore, when the Statist exercises authority arbitrarily, substituting his own ideological preferences for the rational decisions of tens of millions of individuals operating in the free market, he not only creates short-term misery, such as shortages and price spikes, but also long-term misery, because he discourages longer-term investment as well. The individual cannot reasonably know or predict how best to apply his labor and plan for his future. The government ceases to be a reliable force for stability. The oil company cannot be sure how best to direct its resources in developing alternative energy sources. The farmer cannot be sure how best to use his land. The automobile company cannot be sure how best to meet consumer demand. The family cannot be sure how best to invest and save for its own financial security. *Chaotic tyranny* overtakes ordered liberty.

The Conservative understands that if America is to remain a vigorous, civil society in which the individual can continue to improve and progress, the forces arrayed against the free market must be interrupted and their course ultimately reversed. President Abraham Lincoln encapsulated it well when he said, "Property is the fruit of labor . . . property is desirable . . . is a positive good in the world. That some should be rich shows that others may become rich, and hence is just encouragement to industry and enterprise. Let not him who is houseless pull down the house of another; but let him labor diligently and build one for himself, thus by example assuring that his own shall be safe from violence when built."[68]

7

ON THE WELFARE STATE

IF THE STATIST WERE to devise a scheme whereby a grandparent would be stealing future earnings from his own grandchild, would the grandparent consent to such immoral behavior? Yet entitlement programs tend to be intergenerational swindles that threaten the well-being of future generations with massive financial obligations incurred from benefits received by today's generation. The Holy Grail of such programs is Social Security, followed closely by Medicare and Medicaid.

In 2008, David Walker, then the comptroller general of the United States, reported that the total burden in present value dollars of these and other entitlement programs, including the federal government's liabilities, commitments, and contingencies, is about $53 trillion. He added, "Imagine we decide to put aside and invest today enough to cover these promises tomorrow. It would take approximately $455,000 per American household— or $175,000 for every man, woman, and child in the United

States."[1] Medicare and Medicaid spending alone "threaten to consume an untenable share of the budget and economy in the coming decades. The federal government has essentially written a 'blank check' for these programs."[2]

Walker closed his report with this ominous declaration: "Budgets, deficits, and long-term fiscal and economic outlooks are not just about numbers, they are also about values. It is time for all Americans, especially baby boomers to recognize our collective stewardship obligation for the future. In doing so, we need to act soon because time is working against us. We must make choices that may be difficult and unpleasant today to avoid passing an even greater burden on to future generations. Let us not be the generation that sent the bill for its conspicuous consumption to its children and grandchildren."[3]

In the United States, the concept of "social insurance" can be traced back to the beginning of the twentieth century and the work of Columbia University professor Henry Rogers Seager. The ideas expounded by Seager in his work "Social Insurance: A Program of Social Reform" provided a rationale for the modern welfare state. Seager, in turn, was heavily influenced by European models of socialism. As he explained, "For other great sections of the country—the sections in which manufacturing and trade have become the dominant interests of the people, in which towns and cities have grown up, and in which the wage earner is the typical American citizen—the simple creed of individualism is no longer adequate. For these sections we need not freedom from governmental interference, but clear appreciation of the conditions that make for the common welfare, as contrasted with individual success, and an aggressive program of governmental control and regulation to maintain these conditions."[4]

Of course, Seager's advocacy for "an aggressive program of governmental control and regulation" was a radical departure from the nation's founding principles and constitutional system. Yet Seager's views are featured today by the Social Security Administration, which has republished his book in its entirety on its website.[5]

During the Great Depression, President Franklin Roosevelt handpicked a Committee on Economic Security to provide recommendations for alleviating the debilitating effects of the Depression. This committee "recommended that the federal government create a national program that would establish a system of unemployment and old-age benefits and enable the states to provide more adequate welfare benefits."[6] To no one's surprise, Roosevelt quickly acted on the recommendations. When pressing for the passage of his proposed Social Security legislation, Roosevelt stated: "[Economic] security was attained in the earlier days through the interdependence of members of families upon each other and of the families within a small community upon each other. The complexities of great communities and of organized industry make less real these simple means of security. Therefore, we are compelled to employ the active interest of the Nation as a whole through government in order to encourage a greater security for each individual who composes it. . . . This seeking for a greater measure of welfare and happiness does not indicate a change in values. It is rather a return to values lost in the course of our economic development and expansion."[7]

Roosevelt strayed little from Seager's statism. Social Security was a complete change in the relationship between the individual and the federal government. Indeed, it marked one of the earliest and most tangible breaks from American economic and constitutional traditions. And that was Roosevelt's intention. He designed Social Security to entangle the individual in a methodological fiction—the illusion of insurance—that would addict the individual to the opium of entitlements. Roosevelt wanted individuals to believe that they were making "contributions" toward an "insurance program" that would fund a "trust" from which they would receive an "earned benefit." Roosevelt rejected the idea of providing direct welfare payments to the aged and the unemployed because he believed such financing would eventually lose support among those who were taxed to fund it. He insisted that even the lowest wage earner covered by the program pay the same fixed payroll tax as the millionaire.

In response to criticism that the payroll tax was regressive, Roosevelt answered, "Those taxes were never a problem of economics. They are politics all the way through. We put those payroll taxes there so as to give the contributors a legal, moral, and political right to collect their pensions and their unemployment benefits. With those taxes in there, no damn politician can ever scrap my social security program."[8]

The taxes may never have been a problem of economics to Roosevelt, but the economic problem he unleashed on American society has become immense, thanks to the politics he played with the people and their future. And it continues to this day, as he knew it would. Social Security is a widely popular program because the individual has been deceived by the Statist to believe that the government has been prudently and diligently managing his accumulated pension investment in his Social Security account, which he presumes to be funded by his own payroll taxes.

He is led to believe that he is a stakeholder in the system and that he has earned whatever benefits the Statist may cook up. And this view is reinforced with a variety of propaganda tools, including the government regularly sending the individual information through the mail giving him the false impression that his payroll taxes have been set aside for his use upon retirement based on some incomprehensible formula. It is a thorough ruse involving all parts of the government—from the elected branches to the Social Security Administration.

As the late economist Milton Friedman explained,

To preserve the fiction that Social Security is insurance, federal government interest-bearing bonds of a corresponding amount have been deposited in a so-called trust fund. That is, one branch of the government, the Treasury, has given an interest-bearing IOU to another branch, the Social Security Administration. Each year thereafter, the Treasury gives the Social Security Administration additional IOUs to cover the interest due. The only way that the Treasury can redeem its debt to the Social Security Administration is to borrow the money from the public, run a surplus in its other activities or have the Federal Reserve print the money—the same alternatives that would be open to it to pay Social Security benefits if there were no trust fund. But the accounting sleight-of-hand of a bogus trust fund is counted on to conceal this fact from a gullible public." [9]

Stung by critics, the Social Security Administration responds by insisting, "Far from being 'worthless IOUs,' the investments held by the trust funds are backed by the full faith and credit of the U.S. Government. The government has always repaid Social Security, with interest."[10] Of course, lost on the agency is its affirmation that Social Security is not based on any known insurance model. The taxpayers are, after all, "the full faith and credit" behind the U.S. government. The agency holds trillions of dollars in IOUs that the taxpayers have unwittingly assumed and will one day have to make good on, because there are no funded accounts from which individuals can draw. The payroll taxes are spent by the government from the moment they are deducted from the employees' salaries.

Friedman explained: "[Social Security] gives too much attention to 'need' to be justified as return for taxes paid, and it gives too much attention to taxes paid to be justified as adequately linked to need."[11] And because the actual cost of Social Security is masked in insurance terminology, the pressure to increase the adequacy of benefits is constant. Today Social Security pays benefits for retirement; to surviving widows, widowers, children, and dependent parents; and for disability. Further expanding and complicating the program, most are unaware that it now even taps into general tax revenues to pay supplemental income to elderly who are disabled and blind, and cash for food and clothing.

But the Statist has always considered Social Security the foundation for building his counterrevolution. Roosevelt and a relatively small band of cronies, most of whom came from academia and the labor movement and worked their will in the halls of the bureaucracy and Congress—usually out of public view—had wanted to include government-run universal health care as part of Social Security. But it was seen as too politically ambitious even for an overwhelmingly Democratic Congress. They knew if they persisted incrementally, however, manipulating public information and perceptions and adding more and more people to Social Security's rolls, over time they would achieve their ends.

In 1940, about 220,000 people received monthly Social Security checks. By 2004, the number reached 47 million, plus another 7 million received cash payments under Supplemental Security Income.[12] In 2030, Social Security is expected to cover 84 million people and consume 6 percent of the nation's economy, up from 4 percent.[13]

How could the federal government legally force employers and employees to "contribute" to an "insurance" program—particularly a program that was conceived in deceit and punishes their children and grandchildren? The program's constitutionality was challenged and in 1937 the Supreme Court ruled in *Helvering v. Davis* that "the proceeds of both taxes are to be paid into the Treasury like internal-revenue taxes generally, and are not earmarked in any way."[14] Therefore, while Roosevelt was insisting to the public that Social Security was an insurance program based on segregated funds and earned benefits, his lawyers were in Court insisting that it was no such thing—and the Supreme Court played along and betrayed the Constitution.

This clearly is not what the Framers had in mind. In a letter to Edmund Pendleton, a Virginia delegate to the First Continental Congress as well as an influential statesman, James Madison wrote, "If Congress can do whatever in their discretion can be done by money, and will promote the general welfare, the government is no longer a limited one possessing enumerated powers, but an indefinite one subject to particular exceptions."[15]

President Harry Truman picked up where Roosevelt left off. In his State of the Union address in 1948, Truman asserted, "The greatest gap in our social security structure is the lack of adequate provision for the Nation's health. . . . I have often and strongly urged that this condition demands a national health program. The heart of the program must be a national system of payment for medical care based on well-tried insurance principles. . . . Our ultimate aim must be a comprehensive insurance system to protect all our people equally against insecurity and ill health."[16]

In 1965, President Lyndon Johnson, building on the New Deal with his Great Society, used the umbrella of the Social Security Act to establish two massive new entitlement programs—Medicare and Medicaid. As Johnson said when he signed the Medicare bill, "In 1935, when . . . Franklin Delano Roosevelt signed the Social Security Act, he said it was, and I quote him, 'a cornerstone in a structure which is being built but it is by no means complete.' Well, perhaps no single act in the entire administration of the beloved Franklin D. Roosevelt really did more to win him the illustrious place in history he has as did the laying of that cornerstone. . . . And those who share this day will also be remembered for making the most important addition to that structure, and you are making it in this bill, the most important addition that has been made in three decades."[17]

Johnson explained, "Through this new law . . . every citizen will be able, in his productive years when he is earning, to insure himself against the ravages of illness in his old age. This insurance will help pay for care in hospitals, in skilled nursing homes, or in the home. And under a separate plan, it will help meet the fees of doctors."[18]

So Johnson, like Roosevelt, understood the import of deceiving the American people by packaging Medicare's potential costs in the lie of insurance.

Moreover, the economic viability of Medicare was of little consequence to Johnson, who, also like Roosevelt, saw political advantage as a primary consideration. As Wilbur Mills, the chairman of the House Ways and Means Committee, told Johnson when informing him that his committee had passed the Medicare bill, "I think we've got you something that we won't only run on in '66 but we'll run on from here after."[19] And so they have.

Today Medicare covers most people age sixty-five and older, some people under sixty-five with disabilities, and people with end-stage renal disease. It covers most inpatient hospital care, some inpatient skilled nursing home care, some home health care, hospice care, doctors' services, outpatient hospital care, outpatient physical and speech therapy, ambulance services, some medical equipment and supplies, and most prescription drugs.[20] Because Medicare pays providers directly, Medicare users have little incentive to behave cost-efficiently. As in Social Security, virtually everyone "contributes" to the system through a payroll tax, regardless of income level. Medicare is also "funded" through income taxes and relatively small deductible payments. Again, there is no relationship between taxes paid and benefits received and there are no trust funds set aside for future payments.

Nineteen million individuals initially enrolled in Medicare. As of 2006, it covered 43 million people—about 36 million elderly and 7 million disabled.[21] In 2030, Medicare is expected to cover 79 million people and consume 11 percent of the nation's economy, up from 3 percent.[22]

Medicare is running up bigger IOUs, and more quickly, than

even Social Security. In 2008, the Medicare trustees issued a funding warning for the second year in a row, calling attention to the extreme cost pressures in the program resulting from an aging population and escalating costs, and to the excessive use of general tax revenue to pay benefits, and urging Congress to do something about it.[23] "The longer action is delayed, the greater the required adjustments will be, the larger the burden on future generations, and the more severe the detrimental economic impact on our nation."[24] The trustees also estimated that Medicare's unfunded obligation is more than $36 trillion.[25]

Also in 1965, Johnson and the Democratic Congress passed the Medicaid bill. Of course, it, too, was established under the Social Security Act. It is a federal-state program that was originally limited to paying most of the medical bills of low-income people. At first Medicaid covered 4 million individuals. It has since evolved into much more, covering the elderly, people with disabilities, children, and pregnant women—about 51 million people.[26] In 2006, the federal taxpayer paid 57 percent of Medicaid costs. The state taxpayer paid most of the rest.[27] Still, Medicaid consumes on average more than 21 percent of total state spending, making it the largest state expenditure.[28]

Medicare and Medicaid together cover 86 million people (8 million are covered under both programs) or about a quarter of the nation's entire population.[29]

Social Security, Medicare, and Medicaid are built on a family of frauds—the fraudulent concealment of material facts, the fraudulent representation of material facts, and the fraudulent conversion of one's money for another's use. They are a complex mix of taxes, benefits, obligations, and rights from which no indi-

vidual can make much sense and about which the government
sows disinformation and confusion. The "working poor" subsidize
"the wealthy," "the wealthy" subsidize "the working poor," "the
middle class" subsidizes itself as well as "the working poor" and
"the wealthy," and future generations are left paying off the crush-
ing debt created by all of it, since the government spends far
more than it raises. Yet so virtuous are the programs said to be—
pensions for the elderly, compensation for the unemployed, medicine for the sick, and assistance for the disabled—few dare ring
the alarm of looming economic catastrophe that threatens to de-
stabilize the civil society.

The Brookings Institution's Martha Derthick wrote more
than twenty-five years ago about Social Security, and what she
said applies to Medicare and Medicaid as well: "Economic analysts who exposed what they regarded as the myth of social security learned to expect a swift and vigorous response from program
executives, especially if critics were liberals and could therefore
be regarded . . . as 'natural friends' of the system. Then they would
be charged with heresy and made to feel that they were endanger-
ing the system." Jodie Allen, an economist who wrote a critical
article for the *Washington Post* in 1976 ("Social Security: The
Largest Welfare Program"), described the response:

> *I was deluged by calls and letters from the guardians of the social
> security system . . . saying, "Gee, Jodie, we always liked you,
> but how can you say this?" I acted very politely, and I said,
> "Well, what's the matter with this; isn't it true?" And they said,
> "Oh, yes, it's true, but once you start saying this kind of thing,
> you don't know where it's going to end up." Then I came*

to perceive that social security was not a program; it was a religion.[30]

A religion indeed. So much for the Statist's supposed reliance on reason, empiricism, and knowledge.

In 2008, the Congressional Budget Office (CBO) projected that if Social Security, Medicare, and Medicaid go unchanged, by 2082 "the tax rate for the lowest tax bracket would increase from 10 percent to 25 percent; the tax rate on incomes in the current 25 percent bracket would have to be increased to 63 percent; and the tax rate of the highest bracket would have to be raised from 35 percent to 88 percent. The top corporate income tax rate would also increase from 35 percent to 88 percent. Such tax rates would significantly reduce economic activity and would create serious problems with tax avoidance and tax evasion. Revenues will fall significantly short of the amount needed to finance the growth of spending; therefore, tax rates at such levels would probably not be economically feasible."[31]

Despite dire warnings from the CBO, from the former comptroller general of the United States, and from the various trustees that these programs are unsustainable and demand urgent attention, the pillaging of future generations not only continues, but the Statist proposes much more of it in the form of government-run "national health care" or "universal health care." As with Roosevelt and Johnson before him, for today's Statist this is about maximizing power.

It is said by the proponents of government-run health care that 47 million people go without health care in the United States. For example, during the so-called Cover the Uninsured

Week event in 2008, Democratic Speaker of the House Nancy Pelosi issued a statement declaring that this is the "time to reaffirm our commitment to access to quality, affordable health care for every American, including the 47 million who live in fear of even a minor illness because they lack health insurance. . . . In the wealthiest nation on earth, it is scandalous that a single working American or a young child must face life without the economic security of health care coverage."[32] This is more deceit.

In 2006, the Census Bureau reported that there were 46.6 million people without health insurance. About 9.5 million were not United States citizens. Another 17 million lived in households with incomes exceeding $50,000 a year and could, presumably, purchase their own health care coverage.[33] Eighteen million of the 46.6 million uninsured were between the ages of eighteen and thirty-four, most of whom were in good health and not necessarily in need of health-care coverage or chose not to purchase it.[34] Moreover, only 30 percent of the nonelderly population who became uninsured in a given year remained uninsured for more than twelve months. Almost 50 percent regained their health coverage within four months.[35] The 47 million "uninsured" figure used by Pelosi and others is widely inaccurate.

And why is it accepted as fact when Pelosi and other Statists assert that the government can deliver health-care services more efficiently and to all who need them? The British example provides compelling evidence that government-run health care is disastrous, if not deadly, for too many.

In Great Britain, in order to limit waiting times in emergency rooms, the National Health Service has mandated that all patients admitted to a hospital be treated within four hours.[36] However, the inefficiencies of a government-run system cannot be cured by the passage of a law. Consequently, instead of sitting for hours in the hospital waiting room, thousands of patients are forced to wait in ambulances parked outside emergency rooms.[37] Having patients wait in ambulances allows hospitals to use a loophole in delaying care. If the patient is waiting in an ambulance, he cannot be admitted to the hospital and, therefore, does not need to be treated within the four-hour legal time period.

The waiting times for surgeries is a systemic disaster. Patients wait between one and two years to receive hip and knee replacement surgeries.[38] Across specialties, one in seven patients waits more than a year for treatment.[39] Children must travel to the United States to receive certain cancer treatments that are unavailable under Britain's health system.[40]

Like physicians, dentists are employed by the government and required to meet annual treatment quotas. Once the quotas are filled, the dentists are not paid to perform additional work. Recently, dentists in parts of Britain turned away patients and went on vacation because they had met their annual quotas.[41] There are too few public dentists for too many people—even though less than half of adults are registered with public dentists. Those who manage to see a dentist are often given cursory treatment. It is not uncommon for a dentist to spend five minutes on a cleaning. As a result, many Britons are forced to seek dental care abroad. A preferred destination is Hungary.[42]

A recent survey in Britain indicates that as many as one in three family and hospital doctors believes that elderly patients should not be given free treatment if it is unlikely to help them over the long term. Half of the physicians believe that smokers should be denied bypass surgery and a quarter believe the obese should not be eligible for hip replacement surgery.[43]

During her 2008 campaign for the Democratic nomination for president, then-senator Hillary Clinton repeatedly told a shocking tale of a pregnant woman who was about to give birth. Feeling sick, this woman went to her local hospital but was denied care because she lacked health insurance and could not pay a hundred dollars for treatment. Shortly thereafter, the woman was rushed by ambulance to the same hospital, where her baby was stillborn. Several weeks later, the woman died from complications.

A tragic tale? Indeed. But the story was false. The woman was not turned away from the hospital. She had health insurance. She had received obstetrics care from doctors affiliated with the hospital.[44]

It appears that in her search for an example of the heartlessness of the private health-care system, Clinton came up short. But it is not all that difficult to find such examples respecting public health care.

Take Barbara Wagner, who was diagnosed with a recurrence of lung cancer. Her doctors recommended a specific drug to help prolong and improve the quality of her life. However, Barbara is a resident of Oregon and, therefore, part of the state-run Oregon Health Plan. The state refused Barbara's request for the drug, since it does not cover drugs that are meant to prolong the life of individuals with advanced cancer. After all, when the Oregon Health Plan was established in 1994 it "was expressly intended to ration health care." But Oregon also has legalized assisted suicide, and in an unsigned letter from the state, Barbara was informed that the health plan would pay to cover the costs of a doctor to help her kill herself.[45]

Barbara was not ready to have herself killed. However, it seemed she had reached a dead end—until the pharmaceutical company that invented the drug learned of her plight and stepped in to provide Barbara with the medicine free of charge.[46]

Unlike private care, where the difficult, mistaken, or even bad decisions or policies of a single insurance company, hospital, or doctor are usually limited in their societal impact, such governmental decisions and policies have a wide effect on the health-care industry, medical profession, and population of patients. Moreover, the continued centralization of health care decision making ensures further rationing by government fiat with fewer avenues of escape by needy individuals who are denied critical health services. For example, because Medicare and Medicaid, along with other government-run health programs, make the federal government the biggest single purchaser of medicines and medical services, it has an enormous influence on the drugs, medical devices, therapies, and treatment modalities that are available to Americans. It achieves this through formularies: the lists of approved drugs that these programs will pay for. Therefore, those which the government will not approve for payment will generally either not make it to the market or not stay on the market for long, significantly influencing the direction of research and development. The government's payment schemes also affect the nature and quality of doctor and hospital care throughout the marketplace.

The Statist argues that millions of people benefit from these government-run "insurance" programs. Trillions of dollars in government expenditures over the years should result in benefits, particularly for those who receive far more in return than they "contributed" to the system. However, tens of millions more people benefit from private health-care coverage and receive the best medical attention on the face of the earth. Even the government-run programs benefit from the medical advances the private sector is still able to produce; without those advances, the government would have little to ration. And the private sector does not forcibly impoverish future generations with a colossal debt incurred on behalf of current beneficiaries.

Moreover, millions of people might benefit more if they were not forced to participate in government-run "pension" and "insurance" programs. Perhaps they could find less expensive alternatives; invest the taxes deducted from their income to improve their overall financial situation; help pay for food and other necessities during economic setbacks; and hire more employees, who, in turn, can purchase private insurance; or reinvest the dollars into expanding the business. Most individuals know best how to use their own money, which they earned from their own labor. And most individuals are not self-destructive.

Edmund Burke said it well: "What is the use of discussing a man's abstract right to food or to medicine? The question is upon the method of procuring and administering them. In that deliberation I shall always advise to call in the aid of the farmer and the physician, rather than the professor of metaphysics."[47]

But it is the Statist's purpose to make as many individuals as possible dependent on the government. Most Americans are, in fact, satisfied with what they pay for their own health care, the quality of the health care they receive, and their health-care coverage.[48] However, the Statist continues to press for government control over the entire health-care system. He is not satisfied with constraining liberty today. He seeks to reach into posterity to constrain liberty tomorrow.

President Barack Obama's first choice for "Health Care Czar" and Secretary of Health and Human Services was Tom Daschle, who was forced to withdraw his name from nomination due to failure to pay federal income taxes. Nonetheless, Daschle laid out the prototype for nationalizing America's health-care system in his book, *Critical: What We Can Do About the Health Care Crisis*.[49] He proposes the establishment of a Federal Health Board, which would make health-care recommendations binding on all federal health programs. However, as columnist Tony Blankley points out, Daschle writes that "Congress could opt to go further with the Board's recommendations. It could, for example, link the tax exclusion for health insurance to insurance that complies with the Board's recommendation."[50] That would effectively destroy private health care. Daschle proposes that the board be independent from "political pressure"—that is, from public input. Daschle also denigrates technological advances as a "technology arms race" rather than lauding their benefits to patients. And Daschle laments doctors' using their best judgment in providing treatment.[51] No more bothersome insurance regulations, doctor referrals, or co-pays. Daschle's medical Politburo is truly a nightmare circa East Germany 1957: A few well-placed political appointees and their bureaucratic support staff ration health-care resources and decide who gets treatment and who does not and, ultimately, who lives and who dies.

For the Statist, this is the ultimate authority over the individual he has long craved. Once the individual is entrapped, the Statist controls his fate. The individual will be seduced by the notion that he is receiving a benefit from the state when in reality the government is merely rationing benefits. The individual is tethered to the state, literally and utterly reliant on it for his health and survival. Not only does the government have an ownership interest in private property, but it also has one in the physical individual. Rather than the individual making cost-benefit and cost-quality decisions about his own condition, the Statist will do it for him. And the Statist will do it very poorly, as he does most other things.

8

ON ENVIRO-STATISM

SCIENCE, BROADLY DEFINED, IS a door to knowledge. Although the Statist is fond of accusing the Conservative of slamming the door shut, it is actually the Statist who abandons science—just as he abandons the laws of nature, reason, experience, economics, and modernity—when he promotes what can best be characterized as enviro-statism. His pursuit, after all, is power, not truth. With the assistance of a pliant or sympathetic media, the Statist uses junk science, misrepresentations, and fearmongering to promote public health and environmental scares, because he realizes that in a true, widespread health emergency, the public expects the government to act aggressively to address the crisis, despite traditional limitations on governmental authority. The more dire the threat, the more liberty people are usually willing to surrender. This scenario is tailor-made for the Statist. The government's authority becomes part of the societal frame of reference, only to be built upon during the next "crisis."

The pathology of the statist health scare works like this: An event occurs—cases of food contamination are discovered or instances of a new disease arise. Or, as is increasingly the case, government agencies such as the Food and Drug Administration (FDA), the Centers for Disease Control and Prevention (CDC), or the Environmental Protection Agency (EPA), or nonprofit organizations such as the Center for Science in the Public Interest or Sierra Club release a new study identifying a "frightening" new health risk. Urgent predictions are made by cherry-picked "experts" that the media accept without skepticism or independent investigation and turn into a cacophony of fear. Public officials next clamor to demonstrate that they are taking steps to ameliorate the dangers. New laws are enacted or regulations promulgated that are said to limit the public's exposure to the new "risk."

The examples of this pathology are numerous and include such "scares" as alar, sweeteners, bird flu, swine flu, dioxins, *E. coli*, listeria, the Ebola virus, formaldehyde, MTBE (methyl tertiary butal ether), BSE (bovine spongiform encephalopathy), salmonella attached to tomatoes/jalapeño peppers, and CFCs (chlorofluorocarbons). All were blown into huge panics, far beyond the actual scope of any health threat.

Economist George Reisman relates how advances in science make it possible to detect minute levels of contaminants in substances, which are misused in too many cases to destroy products. "The presence of parts per billion of a toxic substance is routinely extrapolated into being regarded as a cause of human deaths. And whenever the number of projected deaths exceeds one in a million (or less), environmentalists demand that the government remove the offending pesticide, preservative, or other alleged bearer of toxic pollution from the market. They do so, even though a level of risk of one in a million is one-third as great as that of an airplane falling from the sky on one's home."[1]

Indeed, the modern environmental movement was founded on one of the most egregious frauds in human history: that dichloro-diphenyl-trichloroethane, or DDT, is a human-killing poison when, in fact, it is a human-saving wonder chemical—a chemical compound developed in 1939 for use as an insecticide. DDT was critical in protecting American soldiers from the typhus epidemic and malaria during World War II.[2] In 1948, Paul Hermann Müller received the Nobel Prize "for his discovery of the high efficiency of DDT as a contact poison against several arthropods."[3]

DDT's usefulness in combating malaria and other insect-borne diseases was unprecedented. San Jose State University professor J. Gordon Edwards, who was a longtime opponent of banning DDT, wrote in 2004: "Hundreds of millions have died from malaria, yellow fever, typhus, dengue, plague, encephalitis, leishmaniasis, filariasis, and many other diseases. In the 14th century the bubonic plague (transmitted by fleas) killed a fourth of the people of Europe and two-thirds of those in the British Isles. Yellow fever killed millions before it was found to be transmitted by *Aedes* mosquitoes. . . . More than 100 epidemics of typhus ravaged civilizations in Europe and Asia, with mortality rates as high as 70 percent. But by far the greatest killer has been malaria, transmitted by *Anopheles* mosquitoes. In 1945, the goal of eradicating this scourge appeared to be achievable thanks to DDT. By 1959, the U.S., Europe, portions of the Soviet Union, Chile, and several Caribbean islands were nearly malaria free."[4]

Journalist and bestselling author Malcolm Gladwell recounted the successful eradication campaigns waged in Italy, Taiwan, the Caribbean, the Balkans, parts of northern Africa, the South Pacific, Australia, and India: "In India, where malaria infected an estimated 75 million and killed 800,000 every year, fatalities had dropped to zero by the early sixties. Between 1945 and 1965, DDT saved millions—even tens of millions—of lives around the world, perhaps more than any other man-made drug or chemical before or since."[5]

A few years ago, *New York Times* editorial page writer Tina Rosenberg explained that "today, westerners with no memory of malaria often assume it has always been only a tropical disease. But malaria was once found as far north as Boston and Montreal. Oliver Cromwell died of malaria, and Shakespeare alludes to it [as 'ague'] in eight plays. Malaria no longer afflicts the United States, Canada and Northern Europe in part because of changes in living habits—the shift to cities, better sanitation, window screens. But another reason was DDT, sprayed from airplanes over American cities and towns while children played outside."[6]

So effective is DDT that in 1970 the National Academy of Sciences announced that "to only a few chemicals does man owe as great a debt as to DDT. In little more than two decades DDT has prevented 500 million human deaths due to malaria that would have otherwise been inevitable."[7]

But in 1962, Rachel Carson, an opponent of pesticides, succeeded in spreading widespread hysteria about DDT's effects on wildlife and especially children. In her book *Silent Spring*, Carson decried the broad use of DDT.[8] As *Reason* science correspondent Ron Bailey wrote, "Carson was . . . an effective popularizer of the idea that children were especially vulnerable to the carcinogenic effects of synthetic chemicals. 'The situation with respect to children is even more deeply disturbing,' she wrote. 'A quarter century ago, cancer in children was considered a medical rarity. Today, more American school children die of cancer than from any other disease.' In support of this claim, Carson reported that 'twelve per cent of all deaths in children between the ages of one and fourteen are caused by cancer.' Although it sounds alarming, Carson's statistic is essentially meaningless unless it's given some context, which she failed to supply. It turns out that the percentage of children dying of cancer was rising because other causes of death, such as infectious diseases, were drastically declining."[9]

It is a sickening irony that Carson's focus on children helped kill the use of DDT when malaria is the cause of death of millions of children living in undeveloped countries. In fact, nowhere in *Silent Spring* did Carson mention that DDT had saved tens of millions of lives, a widely known fact by 1962 but of no apparent import to her or her growing legion of adherents.[10]

The media gobbled up Carson's alarmism. President John Kennedy formed an advisory committee to investigate her claims. Congress held hearings. The Environmental Defense Fund and the Sierra Club brought litigation to pressure the government to ban DDT. Although DDT has never been directly linked to even one human death (Gladwell recounts incidents of test subjects literally lathering themselves with DDT),[11] the EPA, which had been established in 1970, banned DDT in 1972.[12] Its use worldwide soon plummeted because the United States and the United Nations' World Health Organization would no longer provide financial support for the lifesaving chemical's use.[13]

But even the manner in which the EPA banned DDT was an abuse of both the scientific and legal process. An EPA administrative law judge held several months of hearings on DDT's environmental and health risks. In the end, Judge Edmund Sweeney found that "DDT is not a carcinogenic hazard to man . . . DDT is not a mutagenic or teratogenic hazard to man. . . . The use of DDT under the regulations involved here do not have a deleterious effect on freshwater fish, estuarine organisms, wild birds or other wildlife."[14]

However, Sweeney's ruling was rejected by EPA administrator William Doyle Ruckelshaus, who, in 1972, banned it anyway. Ruckelshaus attended none of the hearings and aides reported he had not read the hearing transcript before overruling Sweeney's findings.[15] At the time, Ruckelshaus belonged to the Audubon Society and later joined the Environmental Defense Fund, which, along with the Sierra Club, was a budding organization that brought lawsuits pressing for DDT's ban.[16]

Only recently has the world community begun to revisit the benefits of DDT. In 2006, the World Health Organization announced that it would reverse years of policy and back the use of DDT as a way to control malaria outbreaks.[17] Better late than never, but the ban's human cost has been enormous. In 2002, the American Council on Science and Health reported that 300 million to 500 million people suffer from malaria each year, 90 percent occurring in Africa. It is the number one killer of children there.[18] Overall, the ban has resulted in the deaths of millions.[19]

The EPA and its environmental-group masters conspired in a deliberate and systematic distortion of science, leading to genocide-like numbers of deaths of human beings throughout the undeveloped world. Today the Environmental Defense Fund and the Sierra Club, and scores of similar groups, raise tens of millions of dollars a year to promote their causes in Congress, the bureaucracy, and the courts, are relied on frequently by the media for expert comment, and make no apologies for the consequences of their success in banning DDT. Ruckelshaus, a Republican, rose through the executive branch and has received acclaim for his public service. He currently serves on the boards of numerous corporations and endorsed Barack Obama for president. After her death in 1964, Carson was the recipient of numerous honors and awards. Her childhood home is on the National Register of Historic Places and the home she lived in when she wrote *Silent Spring* was named a National Historic Landmark. There are no landmarks or memorials for those who suffered and perished from the banning of DDT. In the name of protecting wildlife and children, millions of human lives were needlessly sacrificed.

On its website, the group Earth First! declares that it "does not accept a human-centered worldview of 'nature for people's sake.' " It insists that "life exists for its own sake, that industrialized civilization and its philosophy are anti-Earth, anti-woman and anti-liberty . . . To put it simply, the Earth must come first."[20]

Is not man, therefore, expendable? And if he is, is not the suppression of his liberty, the confiscation of his property, and the blunting of his progress at all times warranted where the purpose is to save the planet—or any part of it—from man himself? After all, it would seem that there can be no end to man's offenses against nature if he is not checked at every turn.

National Park Service ecologist David M. Graber, writing in the *Los Angeles Times* in 1989, well articulated the perversity of this view:

We contaminated the planet with atmospheric hydrocarbons and metals beginning in the Industrial Revolution. The Atomic Age wrote another indelible signature in radioisotopes on every bit of the Earth's surface. DDT and its kin appear even in the Antarctic ice. . . . I, for one, cannot wish upon either my children or the rest of Earth's biota a tame planet, a human-managed planet, be it monstrous or—however unlikely—benign. . . . [I am] not interested in the utility of a particular species, or free-flowing river, or ecosystem, to mankind. They have intrinsic value, more value—to me—than another human body, or a billion of them.

Human happiness, and certainly human fecundity, are not as important as a wild and healthy planet. I know social scientists who remind me that people are part of nature, but it isn't true. Somewhere along the line—at about a billion years ago, maybe half that—we quit the contract and became a cancer. We have become a plague upon ourselves and upon the Earth.

It is cosmically unlikely that the developed world will choose to end its orgy of fossil-energy consumption, and the Third World its suicidal consumption of landscape. Until such time as Homo sapiens should decide to rejoin nature, some of us can only hope for the right virus to come along.[21]

If nature has "intrinsic value" then nature exists for its own sake. Consequently, man is not to be preferred over any aspect of his natural surroundings. He is no better than any other organism and much worse than most because of his destructive existence. And so it is that the Enviro-Statist abandons reason for a faith that preaches human regression and self-loathing. And he does so by claiming the moral high ground—saving man from himself and nature from man. Most individuals who are sympathetic to environmental causes are unwitting marks, responsive to the Enviro-Statist's manipulation of science, imagery, and language. Over time, they self-surrender liberty for authority, abundance for scarcity, and optimism for pessimism. "Save the planet!" is the rallying cry that justifies nearly any intrusion by government into the life of the individual. The individual, after all, is expendable.

Who would have thought that the flush toilet would become controversial? It is not only an everyday convenience, which would be enough, but critical to human health. No matter. In 1992, Congress passed the Energy Policy and Conservation Act, outlawing the 3.5-gallon toilet and replacing it with the 1.6-gallon toilet. The purpose was to reduce the use of water. To this day, the mandated change requires users to flush the toilet more often, which hardly saves water. A government that is powerful enough to dictate the flow of water in a toilet is a very powerful government indeed. Some Enviro-Statists even advocate for dry toilets, which are basically dirt pits, especially for the undeveloped world. They claim flush toilets would be "an environmental disaster" if China and the Third World used more of them.[22] Clearly the world's poor are among the Enviro-Statist's most victimized populations.

Today, almost 1.6 billion people use candles and kerosene lamps to light their homes, filling them with smoke and soot and risking fire. In India, where 600 million people live without electricity, Greenpeace campaigned against the incandescent lightbulb because it emits carbon dioxide (apparently forgetting the polluting effect of burning kerosene for light). The lightbulb, they said, is "a hazardous product to everyone," and they dubbed

Philips Electronics, India's major lightbulb producer, a "climate criminal."[23]

In much of the world where the Statist reigns, the nights remain dark. In 2002, Secretary of Defense Donald Rumsfeld commented that "if you look at a picture from the sky of the Korean Peninsula at night, South Korea is filled with lights and energy and vitality and a booming economy. North Korea is dark."[24] Even in the United States, Congress banned incandescent bulbs, by 2014, replacing them with the costlier compact fluorescent lightbulbs—which contain highly toxic *mercury*.

Those without power in India and parts of Asia also suffer through sweltering heat, routinely over 100 degrees. In 2007, the *New York Times* wrung its hands because "the world's atmospheric scientists are concerned that the air-condition boom sweeping across Asia could lead to more serious problems" with the ozone layer.[25] The washing machine, which liberated mostly women from the arduous task of hand-washing clothes, is attacked for its consumption of energy and water and use with laundry detergent.[26] Lawn mowers, chainsaws, leaf blowers, and barbecue grills are all environmental targets.[27]

But the technology most despised by the Enviro-Statist is the automobile because it provides the individual with a tangible means to exercise his independence through mobility. Starting with the Arab oil embargo of 1973, in which the Organization of the Petroleum Exporting Countries cut oil exports to the United States for supporting Israel in the Yom Kippur War, the automobile has been relentlessly demonized as the enemy of the environment.

Among the government's responses to the embargo was the

imposition of Corporate Average Fuel Economy, or CAFE, standards on automobiles in 1975. Its proponents argued that more efficient cars would cut gasoline use, thereby reducing reliance on foreign oil and pollution. But this position was always counterintuitive. More efficient cars reduce the per-mile cost of driving, enabling consumers to pay less than they otherwise would for driving more. In fact, the CAFE standards have not reduced America's importation of oil. In 1970, the United States imported about 20 percent of its oil, compared with over 60 percent today.[28] And while better fuel economy produces more emissions resulting from more driving, CAFE standards were never going to make a significant impact on greenhouse gas emissions. The Heritage Foundation's Charli E. Coon has noted that "cars and light trucks subject to fuel economy standards make up only 1.5 percent of all global man-made greenhouse gas emissions . . ."[29]

Although CAFE standards have failed to reduce gasoline consumption or significantly improve the environment, they have succeeded in killing tens of thousands of human beings. The reason: the laws of physics.

In order to meet the per-gallon fuel efficiency standards set by Congress, the automobile industry has been forced to reduce the size and weight (mass) of vehicles. Consequently, automobiles and light trucks contain more plastic and aluminum than ever before. Their human occupants are more vulnerable to injury and death from most kinds of accidents. The evidence proves the point.

In 1989, analysts at the Brookings Institution and Harvard University estimated that 2,000 to 3,900 lives are lost and 20,000 serious injuries occur each year in traffic accidents resulting from smaller, lighter cars.[30] The Competitive Enterprise Institute examined 1997 traffic fatality data and concluded that CAFE standards caused between 2,600 and 4,500 deaths in 1997.[31] In 1999, USA Today analyzed the statistical link between CAFE standards and traffic fatalities and reported that "46,000 people have died in crashes they would have survived in bigger, heavier cars . . . since 1975."[32] In 2001, a National Academy of Sciences panel reported that the downweighting and downsizing of light vehicles in the 1970s and early 1980s, partly due to CAFE standards, "probably resulted in an additional 1,300 to 2,600 traffic fatalities in 1993.[33]

More Americans are killed and maimed each year from CAFE standards than American soldiers have been killed on the battlefield in Iraq each year. Yet what is the Enviro-Statist's response to this carnage? In 2007, Congress mandated that each automobile manufacturer's passenger vehicles average 35 miles per gallon by 2020, about a 40 percent increase over current standards for cars and trucks. So ingrained in society is the Enviro-Statist's agenda that the effect of this policy on human life was of no consequence to Congress.

For the Conservative, scientific and technological advances, especially since the Industrial Revolution, have hugely benefited mankind. Running water and indoor plumbing enable fresh water to be brought into the home and dirty water to be removed through a system of aqueducts, wells, dams, and sewage treatment facilities; irrigating and fertilizing land creates more stable and plentiful food supplies; harnessing natural resources such as coal, oil, and gas makes possible the delivery of power to homes, hospitals, schools, and businesses and fuel for automobiles, trucks, and airplanes; networks of paved roads promote mobility, commerce, and assimilation; and the invention of medical devices and discovery of chemical substances extend and improve the quality of life.

The Conservative believes that in the context of the civil society, progress and modernity are essential to man's well-being and fulfillment, despite their inevitable imperfections. He rejects the paganlike, antihuman crusade of the Enviro-Statist, which leads to callousness, conformity, and misery. The Conservative also understands that when the independence and liberty of the individual are subject to tyranny posing as righteousness, his right to acquire and retain private property will no longer have standing.

John Adams cautioned that "the moment the idea is admitted into society that property is not as sacred as the laws of God, and there is not a force of law and public justice to protect it, anarchy and tyranny commence."[34]

Today homeowners, farmers, and businesses are subjected to a host of government restrictions and prohibitions that reduce the use and value of their properties, including laws relating to wetlands and endangered species. Among the most far-reaching Enviro-Statist strategies is "smart growth"—where urban planners develop comprehensive zoning initiatives that purport to bring man back into balance with the ecosystem by severely restricting private property rights. And their focus is typically "suburban sprawl." The urban planner's purpose is to force populations into increasingly limited, dense areas; drive cars off the roads and increase use of public transportation or bicycle and pedestrian paths; bring the home and office closer together; and establish a communal existence. This requires severely limiting alternative forms of development and growth outside certain prescribed areas.

But just how problematic is suburban sprawl or, for that matter, development generally? In 2002, the Heritage Foundation's Dr. Ronald D. Utt examined the federal government's land use surveys and concluded, "[A]fter nearly 400 years of unmanaged development and rabbit-like population growth, somewhere between 3.4 percent and 5.2 percent of land in the continental United States has been consumed. . . ."[35]

But what of the heavily urbanized states, which include several of the original colonies? Utt looked at them as well. "In both New York and Virginia, which were settled in the early 1600s, nearly 90 percent of the land is still undeveloped, while in Pennsylvania the share is over 85 percent, and in Maryland it is over 80 percent. In contrast, both New Jersey and Rhode Island's developed shares hover at around one-third of the available land— some of the highest shares in the nation but still leaving both states with about two-thirds of their land undeveloped or in agricultural use."[36]

But the Enviro-Statist has only just begun. His most noxious assault on humankind and the civil society is presented as man-made "global warming." Amazingly, not long ago "global cooling" was all the rage, with warnings of cataclysmic destruction from flooding, famine, and upheaval.

In 1971, Dr. S. I. Rasool, a NASA scientist, insisted that "in the next 50 years, the fine dust man constantly puts into the atmosphere by fossil fuel-burning could screen out so much sunlight that the average temperature could drop by six degrees." Rasool further claimed that "if sustained over several years—five to ten—such temperature decrease could be sufficient to trigger an ice age." Incidentally, in arriving at his conclusions, Rasool used, in part, a computer model created by his NASA colleague and current global warming mystic Dr. James Hansen.[37]

The global cooling alarm was sounded throughout the 1970s. In 1974, *Time* magazine featured an article titled "Another Ice Age?" which cited evidence purporting to show the atmosphere cooling for the previous thirty years. "Telltale signs [of global cooling] are everywhere—from the unexpected persistence and thickness of pack ice in the waters around Iceland to the southward migration of a warmth-loving creature like the armadillo from the Midwest." The article featured opinions from climate experts who suggested that mankind may have been responsible for the earth's cooling. Reid A. Bryson of the University of Wisconsin theorized that dust and "other particles released into the atmosphere as a result of farming and fuel burning may be blocking more and more sunlight."[38]

In 1975, scientists again raised the specter of global cooling. A famous article appearing in *Newsweek* magazine, titled "The Cooling World," concluded, "The central fact is that after three quarters of a century of extraordinarily mild conditions, the earth's climate seems to be cooling down." It continued, "[Meteorologists] are almost unanimous in the view that the trend [of global cooling] will reduce agricultural productivity for the rest of the century." The article cited a survey completed in 1974 by the National Oceanic and Atmospheric Administration (NOAA) revealing a drop of half a degree in the average ground temperatures in the Northern Hemisphere between 1945 and 1968. NOAA scientists had also concluded that "the amount of sunshine reaching the ground in the continental U.S. diminished by 1.3 percent between 1964 and 1972."[39]

Of course, there was no new Ice Age. The "almost unanimous" opinion of weather experts about man-made global cooling was wrong. The Enviro-Statist then swung in the opposite direction, insisting that it is the "almost unanimous" opinion of scientists and other experts that rather than cooling, the earth is actually warming, and man is the culprit once again.

In 2008, the same *Newsweek* that gave weight to the false science of global cooling published an article titled "Global Warming Is a Cause of This Year's Extreme Weather." It wrote mockingly, "It's almost a point of pride with climatologists. Whenever some place is hit with a heat wave, drought, killer storm or other extreme weather, scientists trip over themselves to absolve global warming. No particular weather event, goes the mantra, can be blamed on something so general. Extreme weather occurred before humans began loading up the atmosphere with heat-trapping greenhouse gases such as carbon dioxide. So this storm or that heat wave could be the result of the same natural forces that prevailed 100 years ago—random movements of air masses, unlucky confluences of high- and low-pressure systems—rather than global warming. This pretense has worn thin."[40]

There is no consensus that man has influenced the earth's temperature or that the earth's temperature is warmer now than in past periods. And even if there were a consensus, science is not about majority rule. It either is or it is not.

Massachusetts Institute of Technology professor Richard Lindzen classified "scientific consensus" respecting global warming as "unscientific." He said, "With respect to science, the assumption behind consensus is that science is a source of authority. Rather, it is a particularly effective approach to inquiry and analysis. Skepticism is essential to science; consensus is foreign. When in 1988 *Newsweek* announced that all scientists agreed about global warming, this should have been a red flag of warning. Among other things, global warming is such a multifaceted issue that agreement on all or many aspects would be unreasonable."[41]

But the political appeal of enviro-statism is strong. Former Republican presidential nominee Senator John McCain has insisted, "The debate [about man-made global warming] is over, my friends. Now the question is: what do we do? Do we act, do we care enough about the young people of the next generation to act seriously and meaningfully, or are we going to just continue this debate and this discussion?"[42] Former Republican Speaker of the House Dennis Hastert said, "I believe the debate over global warming is over."[43] Hastert's Republican predecessor, Newt Gingrich, concurred. "My message, I think, is that the evidence is sufficient that we should move towards the most effective possible steps to reduce carbon loading in the atmosphere."[44] Gingrich even said there must be a "green conservatism."[45]

The debate is over? The evidence is sufficient? And this from leading Republicans. But no one has been more demagogic and alarmist, and honored for it by the international community and Hollywood, than former vice president Al Gore. It seems that for Gore and his flock, the separation of church and state ends at environmentalism's edge. Speaking at a Baptist convention, Gore, citing Luke 12:54–57 for scriptural support, argued that it is dishonest for anyone to claim that global warming is merely a theory rather than a scientific fact. "The evidence is there. . . . The signal is on the mountain. The trumpet has blown. The scientists are screaming from the rooftops. The ice is melting. The land is parched. The seas are rising. The storms are getting stronger. Why do we not judge what is right?"[46] And being the prophet that he is, Gore insists that the media stop reporting views that differ from his. "Part of the challenge the news media has had in covering this story is the old habit of taking the on the one hand, on the other hand approach. There are still people who believe that the Earth is flat, but when you're reporting on a story like the one you're covering today, where you have people all around the world, you don't take—you don't search out for someone who still believes the Earth is flat and give them equal time."[47] The media are more than willing to accommodate Gore's commandment. Consider CBS newsmagazine 60 Minutes correspondent Scott Pelley. When asked why his reporting on global warming did not acknowledge the views of skeptics, he replied, "If I do an interview with Elie Wiesel, am I required as a journalist to find a Holocaust denier? This isn't about politics or pseudo-science or conspiracy theory blogs. This is about sound science."[48]

Oh really? President Bill Clinton's undersecretary of state for global affairs, Timothy Wirth, did not quite see it that way. He said, "We've got to ride the global warming issue. Even if the theory of global warming is wrong, we will be doing the right thing, in terms of economic policy and environmental policy."[49] And what is the right thing? Maurice Strong, who was an advisor to former United Nations secretary-general Kofi Annan, provides an answer: "We may get to the point where the only way to save the world will be for the industrial civilization to collapse."[50]

What he really means, of course, is that the world would be saved if the United States collapsed.

The same United Nations has been advocating the case for man-made global warming for several years. In 1988, it established the Intergovernmental Panel on Climate Change (IPCC), which periodically releases reports predicting the end of the world as we know it and insisting its findings are definitive. Dr. Michael Mann, a climatologist, then at the University of Massachusetts, and others conducted an analysis of statistical evidence, from which they concluded that recent temperature increases are "likely to have been the largest of any century during the past 1,000 years" and that the "1990s was the warmest decade and 1998 the warmest year" of the millennium.[51] Mann's results yielded a hockey stick–shaped graph purporting to demonstrate a dramatic spike in global temperatures during the last hundred years. This "hockey-stick effect" has been used to describe global warming. In 2001, the IPCC adopted Mann's findings.[52]

Dr. Edward Wegman, a professor at the Center for Computational Statistics at George Mason University, chair of the National Academy of Sciences' Committee on Applied Theoretical Statistics, and board member of the American Statistical Association, was tasked by a congressional committee to lead a group of experts in examining the hockey-stick evidence. Wegman reported back, "The assessments that the decade of the 1990s was the hottest decade in a millennium and that 1998 was the hottest year in a millennium cannot be supported. The paucity of data in the more remote past makes the hottest-in-a-millennium claims essentially unverifiable." Mann did not have enough historical data to conduct a meaningful study. Wegman added, "There is no

evidence that Dr. Mann or any of the other authors in paleoclimate studies have had significant interactions with mainstream
statisticians."[53] Mann and the other advocates of man-made
global warming did not know how to conduct a correct statistical
analysis, nor did they seek input from legitimate statisticians.
Noting that so many remain convinced of Mann's conclusion despite the inaccuracy of his graph, Wegman said, "I am baffled by
the claim that the incorrect method doesn't matter because the
answer is correct anyway. Method Wrong + Answer Correct =
Bad Science."[54]

Among the most widely cited "authorities" for man-made
global warming is an IPCC panel report produced in 2007. Vaclav
Klaus, president of the Czech Republic, an economist, and a well-
known critic of global warming proponents, has said that the
"IPCC is not a scientific institution: it's a political body, a sort of
non-government organization of green flavor. It's neither a forum
of neutral scientists nor a balanced group of scientists. These people are politicized scientists who arrive there with a one-sided
opinion and a one-sided assignment."[55] A study by the Science
and Public Policy Institute backs Klaus's observation: "The IPCC
is a single-interest organization, whose charter directs it to assume
that there is a human influence on climate, rather than to consider whether the influence may be negligible."[56] As the Heartland Institute notes, "The IPCC's climate science assessment is
dominated by a small clique of alarmists who frequently work
closely with each other outside the IPCC process."[57]

The IPCC continues to allege that the planet is warming, that
the warming is due to an increase in atmospheric carbon dioxide
(CO_2) levels, and that the increased carbon dioxide levels are due

to the burning of fossil fuels. Unless dramatic steps are taken to cut carbon dioxide levels, mankind can expect famine and starvation, rising sea levels and beach erosion, outbreaks of disease, and loss of rain forests: "Warming of the climate system is unequivocal, as is now evident from observations of increases in global average air and ocean temperatures, widespread melting of snow and ice and rising global average sea level." Eleven of the last twelve years (1996–2006) are among the warmest years "in the instrumental record of global surface temperature since 1850." Global average surface temperature has risen, global average sea level has risen, and Northern Hemisphere snow cover has fallen.[58]

"Global atmospheric concentrations of CO_2, methane (CH_4) and nitrous oxide (N_2O) have increased markedly as a result of human activities since 1750 and now far exceed pre-industrial values determined from ice cores spanning many thousands of years." The report further concludes with "very high confidence that the net effect of human activities since 1750 has been one of warming." Moreover, "most of the observed increase in global average temperature since the mid-20th century is very likely due to the observed increase in anthropogenic GHC concentrations [man-made greenhouse gases]." Solar and volcanic activity would have "likely" produced global cooling.[59]

Again, the alarmists' methodologies have come under severe criticism. For example, the surface stations used throughout the United States to measure temperature are subject to distortion. Many readings are influenced by warming caused by nearby buildings, parking lots, and exhaust vents. The temperature station in Marysville, California, is surrounded by an asphalt driveway and air-conditioning units. Its readings have trended up. The tempera-ture station in Orland, California, has not been affected by out-side development. Its readings have trended down.[60] And there are charges that historic CO_2 measurements are intentionally chosen to ensure that the data reflect an increase, such as ignoring CO_2 measurements from the years 1857–1957, which may show higher concentrations of atmospheric CO_2 than exist today.[61]

Even so, does carbon dioxide actually affect temperature lev-els? Dr. Nir Shariv, a top astrophysicist and associate professor at Hebrew University, used to think so, but not anymore: "Like many others, I was personally sure that CO_2 is the bad culprit in the story of global warming. But after carefully digging into the evidence, I realized that things are far more complicated than the story told to us by many climate scientists or the stories regurgi-tated by the media." Shariv notes that "solar activity can explain a large part of the 20th-century global warming" and greenhouse gases are largely irrelevant to the climate. If the amount of CO_2 doubled by 2100, it "will not dramatically increase the global temperature." He added, "Even if we halved the CO_2 output, and the CO_2 increase by 2100 would be, say, a 50% increase relative to today instead of a doubled amount, the expected reduction in the rise of global temperature would be less than 0.5C. This is not significant."[62]

Geologist Dudley J. Hughes puts it another way: "Earth's at-mosphere is made up of several major gases. For simplicity, let us picture a football stadium with about 10,000 people in the stands. Assume each person represents a small volume of one type of gas. . . . Carbon Dioxide [represents] only about 4 parts in 10,000, the smallest volume of any major atmospheric gas."[63]

Plants use carbon dioxide in photosynthesis and exhale oxygen. Humans inhale oxygen to breathe and exhale carbon dioxide. Carbon dioxide is a natural part of the atmosphere—like water vapor. It is not a poison and, therefore, it is not a pollutant. In fact, *water vapor* is by far the earth's most significant greenhouse gas, and without greenhouse gases life could not exist.[64]

There are so many experts who reject the notion of man-made global warming and the historical claims about carbon dioxide they are too numerous to list here. But you would never know it from the media coverage. As the National Center for Public Policy Research reports, in 2008, "Dr. Arthur Robinson of the Oregon Institute of Science and Medicine announced that more than 31,000 scientists had signed a petition rejecting the theory of human-caused global warming. A significant number of scientists, climatologists and meteorologists have expressed doubt about the danger of global warming and whether or not humans are having a significant impact for the worse on the climate."[65] Moreover, numerous experts are now claiming that, once again, the world is cooling.[66]

Phil Chapman, a geophysicist, astronautical engineer, and first Australian to become a NASA astronaut, writes, "All four agencies that track the Earth's temperature—the Hadley Climate Research Unit in Britain, the NASA Goddard Institute for Space Studies in New York, the Christy group at the University of Alabama, and Remote Sensing Systems Inc in California—report that it cooled by about 0.7C in 2007. This is the fastest temperature change in the instrumental record and it puts us back where we were in 1930. If the temperature does not soon recover, we will have to conclude that global warming is over."[67]

But the Enviro-Statist is not deterred. Dr. James Hansen, director of the NASA Goddard Institute for Space Studies and an advisor to Al Gore, and whose early work was used to justify global cooling but who is now the most influential and bombastic high priest of the global warming movement, told Congress in 2008 that "CEOs of fossil energy companies know what they are doing and are aware of long-term consequences of continued business as usual. In my opinion, these CEOs should be tried for high crimes against humanity and nature."[68] Hansen, a master at spinning policy makers and the media, has been effectively challenged by certain of his critics. In 2007, he was forced to revise his figures that showed the hottest decade of the twentieth century was not the 1990s but the 1930s and correct a more recent blunder that showed October 2008 as the hottest on record (scores of temperatures were not based on October readings but on September's numbers, which had been carried over).[69]

But the stampede continues. And the solution is the innocuous-sounding "cap and trade" proposal. For the Conservative, this is the most oppressive economic scheme yet to be advanced by the Statist. The way it would work is that the federal government would dictate greenhouse gas emission levels, with emphasis on carbon dioxide, from fossil fuel use. In a relatively short period of time, the government would mandate the steady reduction of the levels of emissions overall and for particular industries that would be legally permitted. Companies that emit less carbon dioxide (and other gases) than legally allowed could sell the excess allotments to companies that emit more. And the companies that emit more than their allotted amount would face stiff penalties and fines.

How would this be policed?

The federal government would need to create a vast IRS-type bureaucracy to set allowance levels and process permits, collect data, monitor and audit compliance, investigate alleged violations, and ultimately enforce emission standards and levels through penalties, fines, and litigation. Every company that uses fossil fuels and emits carbon dioxide would likely be affected. Individual companies and entire industries would be at the mercy of the federal government's arbitrary determinations. And since the government's role will be the enforcement of its own emission rules and regulations—since there would be no bureaucracy serving as a counterweight, promoting economic growth and free markets—it would be little concerned with the economic consequences of its decisions. Indeed, the stringency of the emission standards would never permit a net excess of emission allowances to offset the amount of emission overages, because to do so would defeat the purpose of the scheme. For individual companies, buying excess carbon emissions would become extremely expensive, resulting in part from price competition. They might be required to reduce production and output, go out of business altogether if their profit margins are tight, or relocate abroad to avoid the emission standards. The jobs lost, wealth destroyed, progress stymied, and resources diverted are of minor import to the Enviro-Statist, who is in a rush to adopt the cap-and-trade scheme.

The Heritage Foundation estimates that one of the more recent cap-and-trade proposals would result in cumulative gross domestic product (GDP) losses of at least $1.7 trillion and could reach $4.8 trillion by 2030; single-year GDP losses of at least $155 billion that realistically could exceed $500 billion; annual job losses exceeding 500,000 before 2030 and that could reach 1,000,000; and the average household paying $467 more each year for natural gas and electricity, or an additional $8,870 to purchase household energy over the period 2012 through 2030.[70]

Just how far would the Enviro-Statist push his man-made, global-warming, anti-carbon-dioxide agenda? Very far. British officials are considering the issuance of a "carbon ration card" to every adult. The card would be used when an individual pays for gasoline, household energy, or airline tickets. Each year, the government would allocate CO_2 credits—with penalties to those who exceed the allotted energy use.[71] California is considering mandating the implementation of "programmable communicating thermostats," or PCTs, in all new homes and new heating/air-conditioning units. The devices allow power authorities to remotely set the air-conditioning or heat levels in your home to a temperature they deem appropriate.[72] And the EPA recently issued an "advanced notice of proposed rulemaking" respecting greenhouse gas emissions from cars and "stationary sources," which could one day include regulating and/or taxing methane emissions from livestock.[73]

But the coming invasion of the home and workplace, the restriction on individual liberty, independence, and mobility, and the deconstruction of America's economic system and impoverishing of the citizenry are justified in the name of a long and growing roster of preposterous assertions that must be listed to be believed.

Dr. John Brignell, retired professor of industrial instrumentation at the University of Southampton in Britain, composed a list[74] of alarmist claims in news reports that man-made global warming causes or has caused:

acne, agricultural land increase, Afghan poppies destroyed, Africa devastated, African aid threatened, Africa in conflict, aggressive weeds, air pressure changes, Alaska reshaped, allergies increase, Alps melting, Amazon a desert, American dream end, amphibians breeding earlier (or not), anaphylactic reactions to bee stings, ancient forests dramatically changed, animals head for the hills, Antarctic ice grows, Antarctic ice shrinks, Antarctic sea life at risk, anxiety treatment, algal blooms, archaeological sites threatened, Arctic bogs melt, Arctic in bloom, Arctic ice free, Arctic lakes disappear, Arctic tundra to burn, Atlantic less salty, Atlantic more salty, atmospheric circulation modified, attack of the killer jellyfish, avalanches reduced, avalanches increased, Baghdad snow, Bahrain under water, bananas grow, beer shortage, beetle infestation, better beer, big melt faster, billion dollar research projects, billion homeless, billions face risk, billions of deaths, bird distributions change, bird visitors drop, birds confused, birds return early, birds driven north, bittern boom ends, blackbirds stop singing, blizzards, blue mussels return, bluetongue, brains shrink, bridge collapse (Minneapolis), Britain Siberian, British gardens change, brothels struggle, brown Ireland, bubonic plague, budget increases, Buddhist temple threatened, building collapse, building season extension, bushfires, business opportunities, business risks, butterflies move north, camel deaths, cancer deaths in England, cannibalism, cataracts, caterpillar biomass shift, cave paintings threatened, childhood insomnia, Cholera, circumcision in decline, cirrus disappearance, civil unrest, cloud increase, cloud stripping, cockroach migration, coffee threatened, cold-climate creatures survive, cold spells (Australia), cold wave (India), computer models, conflict, conflict with Russia, coral bleaching, coral reefs dying, coral reefs grow, coral reefs shrink, cost of trillions, cougar attacks, cradle of civilization threatened, crime increase, crocodile sex, crops devastated, crumbling roads/buildings/sewage systems, cyclones (Australia), cyclones (Myanmar), danger to kids' health, Darfur, death rate increase (US), Dengue hemorrhagic fever, depression, desert advance, desert retreat, disappearance of coastal cities, diseases move north, Dolomites collapse, ducks and geese decline, dust bowl in the corn belt, early marriages, early spring, earlier pollen season, Earth biodiversity crisis, Earth light dimming, Earth lopsided, Earth melting, Earth morbid

fever, Earth on fast track, Earth slowing down, Earth spins faster, Earth to
explode, Earth upside down, Earth wobbling, earthquakes, El Niño intensifica-
tion, erosion, emerging infections, encephalitis, English villages lost, equality
threatened, Europe simultaneously baking and freezing, eutrophication,
evolution accelerating, extinctions (human, civilization, logic, Inuit, smallest
butterfly, cod, ladybirds, pikas, polar bears, gorillas, walrus, whales, frogs,
toads, plants, salmon, trout, wildflowers, woodlice, penguins, a million
species, half of all animal and plant species, mountain species, not polar
bears, barrier reef, leaches), extreme changes to California, fading fall
foliage, fainting, famine, farmers go under, fashion disaster, fever, fir cone
bonanza, fish catches drop, fish downsize, fish catches rise, fish deaf, fish
get lost, fish sex change, fish stocks decline, five million illnesses, flesh
eating disease, flood patterns change, floods, floods of beaches and cities,
flood of migrants, Florida economic decline, flowers in peril, food poisoning,
food prices soar, food security threat, footpath erosion, forest decline, forest
expansion, frog with extra heads, frostbite, frost damage increased, frosts,
fungi invasion, Garden of Eden wilts, genetic diversity decline, gene pools
slashed, giant oysters invade, giant pythons invade, giant squid migrate,
gingerbread houses collapse, glacial earthquakes, glacial retreat, glacial
growth, glacier wrapped, global cooling, global dimming, glowing clouds, golf
Masters wrecked, grasslands wetter, Great Barrier Reef 95% dead, Great
Lakes drop, greening of the North Grey whales lose weight, Gulf Stream
failure, Hantavirus pulmonary syndrome, harmful algae, harvest increase,
harvest shrinkage, hay fever epidemic, health of children harmed, heart
disease, heart attacks and strokes (Australia), heat waves, hibernation
affected, hibernation ends too soon, hibernation ends too late, HIV epidemic,
HIV increasing, homeless 50 million, hornets, human development faces
unprecedented reversal, human fertility reduced, human health improvement,
hurricanes increasing, hurricanes decreasing, hydropower problems,
hyperthermia deaths, ice sheet growth, ice sheet shrinkage, ice shelf
collapse, inclement weather, India drowning, infrastructure failure (Canada),
infectious diseases, inflation in China, insect explosion, Inuit displacement,
Inuit poisoned, invasion of cats, invasion of herons, invasion of jellyfish,
invasion of midges, island disappears, islands sinking, insurance increases,

itchier poison ivy, jets fall from sky, jet stream drifts north, kidney stones, kitten boom, krill decline, lake and stream productivity decline, lake empties, lake shrinking and growing, landslides, lawsuits increase, Loch Ness monster dead, lush growth in rain forests, malaria, mammoth dung melt, maple production advanced, maple syrup shortage, marine diseases, marine food chain decimated, Mediterranean rises, megacryometeors, melanoma, methane emissions from plants, methane burps, methane runaway, melting permafrost, Middle Kingdom convulses, migration, migration difficult (birds), microbes to decompose soil carbon more rapidly, minorities hit, monkeys on the move, Mont Blanc grows, monuments imperiled, moose dying, more bad air days, more raw sewage, mortality increased, mountain (Everest) shrinking, mountains break up, mountains melting, mountains taller, mortality lower, narwhals at risk, national security implications, natural disasters quadruple, new islands, next ice age, NFL threatened, Nile delta damaged, noctilucent clouds, oaks dying, oaks move north, ocean acidification, ocean deserts expand, ocean waves speed up, opera house to be destroyed, outdoor hockey threatened, ozone repair slowed, ozone rise, Pacific dead zone, pest outbreaks, pests increase, phenology shifts, plankton blooms, plankton destabilized, plankton loss, plant viruses, plants march north, polar bears aggressive, polar bears cannibalistic, polar bears drowning, polar bears starve, popcorn rise, porpoise astray, psychiatric illness, puffin decline, railroad tracks deformed, rainfall increase, rape wave, refugees, release of ancient frozen viruses, resorts disappear, rice threatened, rice yields crash, river flow impacted, rivers raised, roads wear out, robins rampant, rocky peaks crack apart, roof of the world a desert, Ross river disease, ruins ruined, salinity reduction, salinity increase, salmonella, satellites accelerate, school closures, sea level rise faster, seals mating more, sewer bills rise, severe thunderstorms, Tuatara sex change, sharks attacking, sharks booming, sharks moving north, sheep shrink, shop closures, short-nosed dogs endangered, shrinking ponds, shrinking shrine, ski resorts threatened, skin cancer, slow death, smaller brains, smog, snowfall increase, snowfall reduction, societal collapse, songbirds change eating habits, sour grapes, space problem, spiders invade Scotland, squid aggressive giants, squid population explosion, squirrels reproduce earlier, storms wetter, storm water drains stressed, street crime to increase, suicide, swordfish in the Baltic, tectonic plate movement, teenage drinking, terrorism, threat to peace, ticks move northward (Sweden), tornado outbreak, tourism decrease, tourism increase, trade barriers, trade winds weakened, transportation threatened, tree foliage increase (UK), tree growth slowed, trees could return to Antarctic, trees in trouble, trees less colorful, trees more colorful, trees lush, tropics expansion, tropopause raised, truffle shortage, turtles crash, turtles lay earlier, vampire moths, Venice flooded, volcanic eruptions, walrus pups orphaned, walrus stampede, wars over water, wars sparked, wars threaten billions, water bills double, water supply unreliability, water scarcity (20% of increase), water stress, weather out of its mind, weather patterns awry, weeds, West Nile fever, whales move north, wheat yields crushed in Australia, wildfires, wind shift, wind reduced, wine—harm to Australian industry, wine industry damage (California), wine industry disaster (US), wine—more English, wine—German boon, wine—no more French, wine passé (Napa), winters in Britain colder, winter in Britain dead, witchcraft executions, wolves eat more moose, wolves eat less, workers laid off, world at war, world bankruptcy, world in crisis, world in flames, yellow fever

The Enviro-Statist's agenda, like much of the Statist's agenda, is increasingly immune from the popular will. In addition to creating and controlling much of the administrative state, the judiciary can usually be counted on to give the Statist's policies legal sanction. Policy becomes the law and the law must be adhered to. Consequently, meaningful debate is, in fact, ended, compliance is mandated, and violators are punished.

Indeed, the Enviro-Statist has relied heavily on litigation to achieve his ends. As Case Western Reserve University Law School professor Jonathan Adler has noted, "To some environmental activists, 'litigation is the most important thing the environmental movement has done' since the 1970s. Most major

federal environmental laws contain so-called citizen-suit provi-
sions, which are actually limited to empowering environmental
groups to bring lawsuits in the public's name. As a result, environmental citizens' suits are now 'a central element of American environmental law."[75] The Sierra Club confers the William O.
Douglas Award—named for one of the most egregiously activist
Supreme Court justices ever—on those "who have made outstanding use of the legal/judicial process to achieve environmental goals."[76]

And in 2007, in a case called *Massachusetts v. EPA*, the Supreme Court delivered the Enviro-Statist one of his biggest victo-
ries. Over the objections of the executive branch and without
support from legislative history, a 5–4 majority of the Court, led
by Associate Justice John Paul Stevens, ruled that the Clean Air
Act covered carbon dioxide and other greenhouse emissions from
automobiles. Moreover, while the Court did not direct the EPA
to regulate the emissions, it left the agency with no real alternative. So, five justices, trained not as scientists but lawyers, determined that carbon dioxide is a pollutant, which the government
must regulate.[77] Just like that, the Enviro-Statist position is now
the law. The imposition of restrictive regulations and lawsuits
against carbon dioxide "polluters" will now expand in ways that
will resonate throughout the economy and society resulting from
the dishonest application of law and science.

In the meantime, the effects of the Enviro-Statist's agenda
continue apace. American society is now threatened by dangerous obstructions to the supply of electricity. *Forbes* magazine's
Mark P. Mills reports that the same policies that have led to supply dislocations and price instability in oil and gas are at work in

the provision of electricity. "By as early as [2009] our demand for electricity will exceed reliable supply in New England, Texas and the West and, by 2011, in New York and the mid-Atlantic region. A failure of a power plant, or a summer-afternoon surge in the load, could make for a blackout or brownout."[78] The reason is that most electricity is generated by coal. "Anticoal activists brag that 59 coal-fired plants were canceled in 2007. Nearly 50 more in 29 states are being contested."[79] Adds Mills, "[Nuclear power plants] produce 20% of U.S. electricity. But there hasn't been a new nuclear plant started in three decades, and licenses are expiring on existing nukes. Opponents are fighting renewal of those licenses."[80] And the future does not look bright. President Obama's secretary of energy, Dr. Steven Chu, a 1997 Nobel laureate in physics, is a global warming advocate openly hostile to the use of coal and a foot-dragger on expanding nuclear power.[81]

The Enviro-Statist poses as the defender of clean air, clean water, penguins, seals, polar bears, glaciers, the poor, the Third World, and humanity itself. But he is already responsible for the death and impoverishment of tens of millions of human beings in the undeveloped world. Now he has moved on to bigger tasks—imposing his societal designs on a free and prosperous people, dictating their lifestyle, controlling their movement, and breaking their spirit.

President Obama's appointment of former Clinton-era EPA administrator Carol M. Browner as his "global warming czar" makes clear his intentions. Browner, who is responsible for coordinating the administration's environmental and energy policies, was recently one of fourteen leaders of the Socialist International's Commission for a Sustainable World Society. As the *Washing-*

ton Times explains, the commission "calls for global governance and says rich countries must shrink their economies to address climate change." It also seeks "binding and punitive limits on greenhouse gas emissions."[82]

New York Times columnist Thomas Friedman, author of *Hot, Flat, and Crowded: Why We Need a Green Revolution—and How It Can Renew America*, recently expressed his frustration with the slow pace of the enviro-statism agenda by wishing that "our government could get its act together and launch a green revolution with the same persistent focus, stick to the same direction that China does through authoritarian means."[83]

China? This is the same regime that sends political opponents to reeducation camps or worse and has one of the dirtiest environments on the planet.

The Enviro-Statist declares his allegiance to science and knowledge when, in fact, his only faith is to his ideology. Now that climate models suggest a slight global cooling (again?), his terminology changes from "man-made global warming" to "man-made climate change." Henceforth, Mother Nature's doings will be mankind's responsibility no matter what science reveals. The Enviro-Statist has declared war on the civil society and he is impatient.

9

ON IMMIGRATION

THE STATIST'S ARGUMENT FOR "comprehensive immigration reform" reduces to this: America is a nation of immigrants. The founding and settling of the nation came about because of immigrants who braved dangers to come to this country and risked everything to build the prosperity we enjoy today. Certainly this is true, as far as it goes.

Of course, to say this is a nation of immigrants is to say every nation is a nation of immigrants. Mexico, the source of most immigrants in the United States today, is a nation of Spanish (and other) immigrants. The implication is, however, that both legal and illegal immigration, no matter how extensive, is another moral imperative justifying the transformation of the civil society. This is not so.

Once again, the Declaration of Independence provides guidance on this issue. It states, in relevant part, that "to secure these [unalienable] rights, Governments are instituted among Men, deriving their just powers from the consent of the governed." Moreover, "it is the Right of the People to alter or abolish [the government], and to institute new government, laying its foundation on such principles and organizing its powers in such form, as to them shall seem most likely to effect their safety and happiness. . . ."

Have the governed—American citizens—consented to the current state of legal and illegal immigration in the nation? Do current immigration policies and enforcement practices affect the safety and happiness of the people?

The Statist insists that, in particular, the twenty-first-century immigrant in the United States is the spiritual heir of the immigrants who helped build the nation. His motives are as noble and his ambitions as honorable as those of the Founders. To deny him access to America's bounty and freedom displays an un-American meanness of character and is a renunciation of America's heritage. Even worse, the Statist portrays the immigrant as universally more virtuous than the citizen. He is said to aspire to and, indeed, achieve a higher position of worthiness than the citizen, for he is doing "jobs Americans won't do," "is a person of faith," and "a strong family man." The citizen is said to owe his sustenance to the immigrant, who builds his home, maintains his property, harvests his food, raises his children, goes to war, etc. Therefore, even the illegal immigrant deserves a privileged status in society in the sense that his lawbreaking is said to be of personal necessity and societal value. Consequently, he must be urged "out of the shadows" and into the light. He must be celebrated as a role model. And his virtuousness must be rewarded with citizenship.

For the Conservative, this is a truly odd formulation, since it demeans the citizen and his paramount role in American society. It is the community of citizens who consent to be governed and for whom the government exists. The principal responsibility of the government is to the citizen. Otherwise, the government ceases to be legitimate. To say that the citizen, who is in fact primarily responsible for the nation's character and the culture to which the alien immigrates, is less valuable to American society than the immigrating alien is nonsensical.

No society can withstand the unconditional mass migration of aliens from every corner of the earth. The preservation of the nation's territorial sovereignty, and the culture, language, mores, traditions, and customs that make possible a harmonious community of citizens, dictate that citizenship be granted only by the consent of the governed—not by the unilateral actions or demands of the alien—and then only to aliens who will throw off their allegiance to their former nation and society and pledge their allegiance to America.

Claremont Institute senior fellow and California State University professor Edward J. Erler, reflecting Aristotle's observation, writes, "A radical change in the character of the citizens would be tantamount to a regime change just as surely as a revolution in its political principles."[1] The government, therefore, is not only justified but obligated to qualify immigration to those most likely to contribute to the well-being of the civil society, and to create the conditions in which aliens of differing backgrounds can be absorbed into the American culture.

In 1965, as part of the Great Society, the Statist did, in fact, lay the foundation for radically altering the character of American society and the relationship of the governed to their government. When he signed the Hart-Celler Act, President Lyndon Johnson said, "This bill that we will sign today is not a revolutionary bill. It does not affect the lives of millions. It will not reshape the structure of our daily lives, or really add importantly to either our wealth or our power."[2] And during the debate over the bill on the floor of the Senate, Senator Ted Kennedy claimed, "First, our cities will not be flooded with a million immigrants annually. Under the proposed bill, the present level of immigration remains substantially the same. . . . Secondly, the ethnic mix of this country will not be upset. . . . Contrary to the charges in some quarters, [the bill] will not inundate America with immigrants from any one country or area, or the most populated and economically deprived nations of Africa and Asia."[3]

Johnson, Kennedy, and the other Statists were wrong, and it is hard to believe they were not intentionally deceiving the public. In 1964, Republican vice presidential candidate Representative William Miller well understood the overall increase in immigration that would result from the 1965 act: "We estimate that if the President gets his way, and the current immigration laws are repealed," he said, "the number of immigrants next year will increase threefold and in subsequent years will increase even more."[4]

The bill abolished the decades-old policy of national quotas, which was said to be discriminatory because it favored immigrants from Europe (especially the United Kingdom, Ireland, and Germany) over the Third World. Thus it increased immigration levels from each hemisphere, setting in motion a substantial increase in immigration from Latin America, Asia, and Africa—to the detriment of previously favored aliens from Europe. The bill also introduced, for the first time, a system of *chain migration*, which, as the Center for Immigration Studies notes, "gave higher preference to the relatives of American citizens and permanent resident aliens than to applicants with special job skills."[5] Those who receive preference for admission include unmarried adult sons and daughters of United States citizens, spouses and children and unmarried sons and daughters of permanent resident aliens, married children of United States citizens, and brothers and sisters of United States citizens over the age of twenty-one.[6]

Consequently, the historical basis for making immigration decisions was radically altered. The emphasis would no longer be on the preservation of American society and the consent of the governed; now aliens themselves would decide who comes to the United States through family reunification. With the elimination of national quotas and the imposition of chain migration, aliens immigrating to the United States were poorer, less educated, and less skilled than those who had preceded them—a pattern that continues to this day. The Manhattan Institute's Steven Malanga writes that the first great migration a hundred years ago attracted "Jewish tailors and seamstresses who helped create New York's garment industry, Italian stonemasons and bricklayers who helped build some of our greatest buildings, German merchants, shopkeepers, and artisans—all [of whom] brought important skills with them that fit easily into the American economy. Those waves of immigrants . . . helped supercharge the workforce at a time when the country was going through a transformative economic expansion that craved new workers, especially in cities." Moreover, as a result of the 1965 law, "[l]egal immigration . . . soared from 2.5 million in the 1950s to 4.5 million in the 1970s to 7.3 million in the 1980s to about 10 million in the 1990s."[7]

Furthermore, as political and economic circumstances in the Third World deteriorated, particularly in Mexico and other parts of Latin America, Asia, and Africa, the egalitarian nature of the 1965 law and the growing American welfare state also encouraged the unprecedented and *illegal* migration of millions of additional destitute and uneducated aliens to the United States. So, too, did the 1986 Immigration Reform and Control Act's grant of one-time amnesty to about 3 million illegal aliens, which was conditioned on border security and immigration enforcement that never materialized under subsequent administrations.[8]

The late author Theodore White, who was no conservative, wrote that "the immigration Act of 1965 changed all previous patterns, and in so doing, probably changed the future of America. . . . [It] was noble, revolutionary—and probably the most thoughtless of the many acts of the Great Society."[9]

In the 1960s, Cesar Chavez, one of the founders of the United Farm Workers (UFW) union, vehemently opposed illegal immigration, arguing it undermined his efforts to unionize farm workers and improve working conditions and wages for American citizen workers. The UFW even reported illegal immigrants to the Immigration and Naturalization Service.[10] In 1969, Chavez led a march, accompanied by Ralph Abernathy, president of the Southern Christian Leadership Conference, and Senator Walter Mondale, along the border with Mexico, protesting the farmers' use of illegal immigrants.[11]

But most unions soon changed course and today they lobby to confer amnesty and ultimately citizenship on illegal aliens. These include: American Federation of Labor–Congress of Industrial Organizations; American Federation of State, County and Municipal Employees; Farm Labor Organizing Committee; Hotel Employees and Restaurant Employees International Union; Laborers' International Union of North America; Service Employees International Union; Union of Needletrades, Industrial and Textile Employees; United Farm Workers; and United Food and Commercial Workers.

The unions view the large influx of both legal and illegal immigrants as a new source of political clout that favors their allies in the Democratic Party and potentially adds membership to their own dwindling numbers. They came to the same realization as historian Samuel Lubell, who noted that the voting-age children of the first great migration constituted "the big-city masses [who] furnished the votes which re-elected [Franklin] Roosevelt again and again—and, in the process, ended the traditional Republican majority in this country."[12] And there can be no doubt, as a practical matter, that the Statist's benefits-for-votes promises is an attractive albeit destructive enticement. Despite President George W. Bush's and Senator John McCain's long record of advocacy for more legal immigration and amnesty for illegal aliens, it was not enough to compete with the Statist's agenda. In 2004, 44 percent of Hispanics, for example, voted for Bush for president and 53 percent voted for John Kerry. In 2008, 31 percent of Hispanics voted for McCain for president and 67 percent voted for Barack Obama.[13]

The Statist tolerates the illegal alien's violations of working, wage, and environmental standards, because the alien's babies born in America are, under the current interpretation of the Fourteenth Amendment to the Constitution, treated as United States citizens. And under the Hart-Celler Act, upon turning twenty-one years of age, the child can sponsor additional family members for citizenship. From the Statist's perspective, the pool of future administrative state constituents and sympathetic voters is potentially bottomless.

But does the Fourteenth Amendment grant automatic citizenship to the children of illegal aliens? The relevant part of the amendment reads that "all persons, born or naturalized in the United States, *and subject to the jurisdiction thereof*, are citizens of the United States."[14] This language requires more than birth within the United States. The amendment's purpose was to grant citizenship to the emancipated slaves, who were born in the United States and owed sole allegiance to it. Native Americans who were also subject to tribal jurisdiction were excluded from citizenship. There is no legislative history supporting the absurd proposition that the Fourteenth Amendment was intended to empower illegal alien parents to confer American citizenship on their own babies merely as a result of their birth in the United States. Foreign visitors and diplomats are not subject to American jurisdiction. Illegal aliens are subject to the jurisdiction of their home country, as are their children, whether they are born in their home country or the United States.

The combination of intended and unintended consequences, and legal and illegal immigration, is transforming American society. Using the U.S. Census Bureau's data collected in March 2007, the Center for Immigration Studies reported, in part:

- The nation's immigrant population (legal and illegal) reached a record of 37.9 million in 2007.
- Immigrants account for 1 in 8 U.S. residents, the high-

est level in eighty years. In 1970 it was 1 in 21; in 1980 it was 1 in 16; and in 1990 it was 1 in 13.

- Overall, nearly one in three immigrants is an illegal alien. Half of Mexican and Central American immigrants and one-third of South American immigrants are illegal.

- Of adult immigrants, 31 percent have not completed high school, compared to 8 percent of natives. Since 2000, immigration increased the number of workers without a high school diploma by 14 percent, and all other workers by 3 percent.

- The proportion of immigrant-headed households using at least one major welfare program is 33 percent, compared to 19 percent for native households.

- The poverty rate for immigrants and their U.S.-born children (under 18) is 17 percent, nearly 50 percent higher than the rate for natives and their children.

- 34 percent of immigrants lack health insurance, compared to 13 percent of natives. Immigrants and their U.S.-born children account for 71 percent of the increase in the uninsured since 1989.

- Immigration accounts for virtually all of the national increase in public school enrollment over the last two decades. In 2007, there were 10.8 million school-age children from immigrant families in the United States.[15]

The Pew Hispanic Center estimates that 9 *percent of the population of Mexico* was living in the United States in 2004. Fifty-seven percent of all illegal immigrants are Mexican. Another 24 percent are from other Latin American countries. Fifty-five percent of all Mexicans in the United States are here illegally.[16] By 2050, Hispanics will be between 29 percent and 32 percent of the nation's population.[17]

Washington Post columnist Robert J. Samuelson analyzed the Census Bureau's annual statistical report on poverty and household income for 2006 and found, among other things, that "there were 36.5 million people in poverty. That's the figure that translates into the 12.3 percent poverty rate. In 1990, the population was smaller, and there were 33.6 million people in poverty, a rate of 13.5 percent. The increase from 1990 to 2006 was 2.9 million people (36.5 million minus 33.6 million). Hispanics accounted for all of the gain."[18]

Samuelson explained that "from 1990 to 2006, the number of poor Hispanics increased 3.2 million, from 6 million to 9.2 million. Meanwhile, the number of non-Hispanic whites in poverty fell from 16.6 million (poverty rate: 8.8 percent) in 1990 to 16 million (8.2 percent) in 2006. Among blacks, there was a decline from 9.8 million in 1990 (poverty rate: 31.9 percent) to 9 million (24.3 percent) in 2006. White and black poverty has risen somewhat since 2000 but is down over longer periods." He added, "Only an act of willful denial can separate immigration and poverty. The increase among Hispanics must be concentrated among immigrants, legal and illegal, as well as their American-born children. Yet, this story goes largely untold."[19]

The Manhattan Institute's Heather Mac Donald points to another problem with the mass Hispanic migration to the United States—the "fertility surge" among unwed Hispanic women, particularly teenage girls. "Hispanic women have the highest unmarried birthrate in the country—over three times that of whites and Asians, and nearly one and a half times that of black women." Moreover, "the rate of childbirth for Mexican teenagers, who come from by far the largest and fastest-growing immigration population, greatly outstrips every other group."[20]

Education is another problem as immigrants bring different cultural attitudes and their sheer numbers overwhelm many school systems. In Mexico, a child is legally required to attend school up through the eighth grade. In part, this is why 32 percent of all illegal immigrants and 15 percent of legal immigrants have not completed the ninth grade. Only 2 percent of natives of the United States have not. Nearly 31 percent of adult immigrants do not have a high school diploma. Eight percent of United States natives do not.[21]

Local public school systems are struggling with the consequences of the federal government's policies. According to the Pew Hispanic Center, one out of every five students in 2006 was Hispanic. Between 1990 and 2006, Hispanic students accounted for nearly 60 percent of the total increase in students attending public schools. And by 2050, Pew predicts that the Hispanic school-aged population will increase by 166 percent. Hispanic children are expected to make up the majority of public school students by 2050.[22]

The enormity of migration to the United States also discourages the use of English and encourages the establishment of ethnic enclaves. The 2007 Census Bureau's American Community Survey found that more than 55 million individuals in the United States speak a language other than English at home. Of these people, more than 34 million speak Spanish at home. More than

16 million of the Spanish-speaking individuals speak English "less than very well."[23] Furthermore, in 2000, 43 percent of Hispanics lived in neighborhoods with Hispanic majorities, up from 39 percent in 1990.[24]

Of course, the administrative state has prospered hugely from the immigration anarchy the Statist has unleashed. The Heritage Foundation's Robert Rector writes that "historically, Hispanics in America have had very high levels of welfare use. . . . [In recent years], Hispanics were almost three times more likely to receive welfare than non-Hispanic whites. Putting together the greater probability of receiving welfare with the greater cost of welfare per family means that, on average, Hispanic families received four times more welfare per family than white non-Hispanics. . . . Welfare use can also be measured by immigration status. In general, immigrant households are about 50 percent more likely to use welfare than native-born households. Immigrants with less education are more likely to use welfare."[25]

In 2008, a Manhattan Institute study, "Measuring Immigrant Assimilation in the United States," found that the current level of assimilation of all recent immigrant groups is lower than at any time during the first great migration early in the twentieth century. While some ethnic groups assimilated better than others, and for different reasons, Mexicans were the least assimilated overall and were assimilating at the slowest rate. Even those Mexicans who came to the United States as children (aged five and younger) show discouraging trends. They are more likely than other ethnic immigrant groups to be teen mothers or incarcerated: "Mexican adolescents are imprisoned at rates approximately 80 percent greater than immigrant adolescents generally."[26]

Unlike past waves of migration to the United States, which had identifiable beginnings and ends, the current influx is not a wave but an ongoing tsunami that began more than forty years ago and, apart from temporary slowdowns resulting mostly from a cooling American economy and haphazard enforcement of immigration laws, is likely to continue in the decades ahead.

The citizenry was assured that the 1965 act would not produce what it in fact has now produced. Yet, there is no serious effort to repeal chain migration or even call a temporary halt to it. The Statist does not allow the nation time to try to absorb the aliens who are already here before encouraging more to follow. Federal and state laws and policies that grant de facto citizenship to illegal aliens—the lax enforcement of employer sanctions and the granting of driver's licenses, in-state college tuition, hospital care, mortgages, and public education—send a signal to aliens around the world that America is not serious about immigration enforcement. And when numerous cities and towns designate themselves "sanctuary cities" and order their employees and local law enforcement officers not to cooperate with federal immigration authorities, the rule of law is flouted by public officials and illegal aliens alike. America has never experienced or tolerated anything like this.

Moreover, rather than Americanize aliens and use public and private institutions to inculcate them with the virtues of American culture, language, mores, history, traditions, and customs, the Statist is cultivating a *cultural relativism* in which the cultures from which the aliens fled are given equal accord with the American culture. But all cultures are not equal, as evidenced, in part, by the alien fleeing his own country for the American culture and the American citizen staying put. It is normal and healthy for ethnic groups to celebrate their diverse heritages—Columbus Day, St. Patrick's Day, etc.—and they have since the nation's founding. Most large cities have a Chinatown, Little Italy, and Germantown. In many of these ethnic neighborhoods, the "old language" is still spoken, especially among the older generations. But neither the heritage nor home language of the individual has ever competed with the American culture for dominance. The history of immigration in the United States up to now has been of assimilation.

In his 1796 Farewell Address to the nation, George Washington explained it this way:

> *Citizens, either by birth or choice, of a common country, that country has the right to concentrate your affections. The name of American, which belongs to you, in your national capacity, must always exalt the just pride of Patriotism, more than any appellation derived from local discriminations.*[27]

For more than two centuries, individuals with diverse backgrounds have come together to form a national "melting pot" and harmonious society sustained by allegiance to the country and its founding principles. But today's open-ended mass migration, coupled with the destructive influences of biculturalism, multiculturalism, bilingualism, multilingualism, dual citizenship, and affirmative action, have combined to form the building blocks of a different kind of society—where aliens are taught to hold tightly to their former cultures and languages, balkanization grows, antagonism and conflict are aroused, and victimhood is claimed at perceived slights. If a nation does not show and teach respect for its own identity, principles, and institutions, that corrosive attitude is conveyed to the rest of the world, including newly arriving aliens. And if this is unchecked, the nation will ultimately cease to exist.

Dr. Samuel P. Huntington, who served as chairman of Harvard's Government Department and its Academy for International and Area Studies, observed that "the persistent inflow of Hispanic immigrants threatens to divide the United States into two peoples, two cultures, and two languages. . . . The United States ignores this challenge at its peril." He argued that "Mexican immigration differs from past immigration and most other contemporary immigration due to a combination of six factors: contiguity, scale, illegality, regional concentration [in the Southwest], persistence, and historical presence." The consequences, he believed, are stark: "Demographically, socially, and culturally, the *reconquista* [re-conquest] of the Southwest United States by Mexican immigrants is well underway."[28]

The United States is already a bilingual nation. Government at all levels and a growing list of private concerns do business in both English and Spanish. And Spanish is the predominant language in communities throughout the country. This is a destructive condition. St. Augustine observed: "When men cannot communicate their thoughts to each other, simply because of difference of language, all the similarity of their common human nature is of no avail to unite them in fellowship."[29] Alexis de Tocqueville made the same point: "Language is perhaps the strongest, perhaps most enduring link which unites men."[30]

How can the alien participate fully in American society if

he does not share the language that binds citizen to citizen? How can he acquire better skills, pursue higher learning, or interact effectively in the marketplace if he does not speak English? How can he assess the benefit of entering into contracts or other legal arrangements if he cannot understand the terms and conditions to which he commits himself? And most important, how can the alien comprehend the nation's founding principles and pledge allegiance to them if he cannot be sure of their intended meaning? Clearly neither the alien nor the civil society is the better.

Yet proponents of unrestricted immigration vilify those who attempt to promote a common language. Raul Yzaguirre, who for thirty years was president and CEO of the group National Council of La Raza, reportedly said that "U.S. English is to Hispanics as the Ku Klux Klan is to blacks."[31] Funded, in part, by the Ford Foundation and numerous other corporate and nonprofit contributions, La Raza—meaning "the race" in English—works tirelessly against the assimilation of legal Hispanic aliens into American society and for the continuation of illegal Hispanic migration into the country. Writing in *FrontPage Magazine*, John Perazzo disclosed that La Raza

- views the United States as an irredeemably racist nation
- favors racial and ethnic preferences for minorities in the workplace and in higher education
- supports open borders and amnesty for all illegal aliens
- supports the DREAM Act, which is designed to allow illegal aliens to attend college at the reduced tuition rates normally reserved for in-state legal residents

- advocates "reform" that would give illegal aliens full access to taxpayer-funded health care services
- characterizes any reduction in government assistance to illegal border-crossers as "a disgrace to American values"
- supports access to driver's licenses for illegal aliens
- supports voting rights for illegal aliens
- opposes the Aviation Transportation and Security Act requiring that all airport baggage screeners be U.S. citizens
- opposes the Clear Law Enforcement for Criminal Alien Removal Act, which would empower state and local police to enforce federal immigration laws
- opposes the REAL ID Act, which requires that all driver's license and photo ID applicants be able to verify they are legal residents of the United States, and that the documents they present to prove their identity are genuine.[32]

Despite this radical agenda, which has been consistently rejected by American voters, leaders of this movement are welcomed at the highest levels of power. Hillary Clinton appointed Yzaguirre as cochair of her presidential campaign and assigned him to lead her outreach to Hispanics. McCain was honored by his group in 1999. President Obama appointed Cecilia Muñoz, a senior vice president of La Raza, as director of his Office of Intergovernmental Affairs. There are a multitude of such groups and individuals welcome at the highest levels of the government, where they exert influence on public policy decisions. McCain also appointed an individual to the top ranks of his presidential campaign—Juan Hernandez, who was born in America but holds dual citizenship with Mexico—as his Hispanic outreach director. Hernandez once held the same position for Mexico's former president, Vicente Fox. In 2001, Hernandez, speaking of Mexican-Americans, said that "I want the third generation, the seventh generation, I want them all to think 'Mexico first.' "[33]

The U.S. Chamber of Commerce and other business interests in the United States are economic enablers for this mentality. It is hard to believe that the Chamber uses its considerable clout with Congress to urge the importation of even more low-skilled and unskilled laborers. After all, who else will cut lawns, wash dishes, and pick lettuce? Of course, Americans will, if the price is right. The Hoover Institution's Thomas Sowell writes, "Virtually any job is a job that Americans will not take if the pay is low enough. Nor is there any reason for pay to rise if illegal immigrants are available at low pay."[34] Center for Immigration Studies executive director Mark Krikorian adds, "If the supply of foreign workers were to dry up . . . employers would respond to this new, tighter, labor market in two ways. One, they would offer higher wages, increased benefits, and improved working conditions, so as to recruit and retain people from the remaining pool of workers. At the same time, the same employers would look for ways to eliminate some of the jobs they now are having trouble filling. The result would be a new equilibrium, with blue-collar workers making somewhat better money, but each one of those workers being more productive." He adds, "by holding down natural wage growth in labor-intensive industries, immigration serves as a subsidy for low-wage, low-productivity ways of doing business, retarding technological progress and productivity growth."[35]

American immigration policy also has the perverse effect of upholding the dysfunctional status quo in Mexico. Johns Hopkins University professor Steve H. Hanke argues that Mexico's labor policies mirror those of communist Yugoslavia under Marshal Tito. "Rather than modernize the economy, Mexico's politicos have embraced a Tito-inspired strategy: When incapable of fostering productive jobs, export the labor force. As a result, over 27 percent of Mexico's labor force [was] working in the U.S. [in 2006] and these workers are sending home $20 billion in remittances. That equals one-third of the total wage earnings in the formal sector of the Mexican economy and 10% of Mexico's exports."[36]

The law of supply and demand through the importation of low-skilled and unskilled labor has had exactly the consequences Cesar Chavez originally feared—namely, it reduces the availability of entry-level or low-skill jobs for Americans and drives down wages for unskilled American workers who find jobs. Harvard University professor George J. Borjas found that "by increasing the supply of labor between 1980 and 2000, immigration reduced the average annual earnings of native-born men by an estimated $1,700 or roughly 4 percent." In addition, "the negative effect on native-born black and Hispanic workers is significantly larger than on whites because a much larger share of minorities are in direct competition with immigrants."[37]

The *American Thinker*'s Lee Cary wondered what demand might exist for unskilled labor in the future. He looked at U.S. Department of Labor statistics and concluded it was not very promising. "From 2006 to 2016, the portion of Hispanics in the labor force is projected to grow from 13.7 percent to 16.4 percent.

Meanwhile, the vocational supersectors expected to experience the greatest growth ('education and health services' and 'professional and business services') will generally require, at a minimum, a high-school education. Supersectors where unskilled Hispanics experience the highest level of employment today, construction and agriculture, are expected to grow a modest 10.6 percent and decline 2.8 percent, respectively."[38] In a modern economy with growing emphasis on education and higher skills, the surplus of unskilled foreign labor will further strain and expand social services while keeping wages low for those who find entry-level and low-skill jobs.

Although certain businesses related to agriculture, hotel and restaurant services, lawn services, and construction may benefit from an endless supply of poor and unskilled foreign labor willing to work below the minimum wage and without the panoply of benefits employers are compelled to provide for legal employees, the rest of society is forced to subsidize these businesses by paying for benefits the foreign laborers and their families receive through public education, health care, and a menu of welfare state offerings. For this reason, Milton Friedman declared, "It's just obvious you can't have free immigration and a welfare state."[39] And, again, the proportion of immigrant-headed households using at least one major welfare program is 33 percent. As Professor Borjas has said, "Being without work [in the United States] is still far better for most people than being employed in Central America."[40]

Robert Rector notes, "In FY 2004, low-skill immigrant households received $30,160 per household in immediate [government] benefits and services (direct benefits, means-tested benefits, education, and population-based services). In general, low-skill immigrant households received about $10,000 more in government benefits than did the average U.S. household, largely because of the higher level of means-tested welfare benefits received by low-skill immigrant households. In contrast, low-skill immigrant households paid only $10,573 in taxes in 2004. Thus, low-skill immigrant households received nearly three dollars in immediate benefits and services for each dollar in taxes paid."[41]

The late Minnesota senator and Democratic presidential candidate Eugene McCarthy wrote, "The United States cannot regain its competitive standing in the world by importing low wage workers from other countries. On the one hand, it engenders conditions this country cannot and should not tolerate. . . . On the other hand, in the modern age a nation's wealth and prosperity is secured by high worker productivity and capital investment, not by the availability of low-wage labor."[42]

There are other costs to society resulting from open immigration, including crime. The National Youth Gang Survey 1999–2001, published by the Department of Justice, reported that approximately half of all gang members were Hispanic/Latino in 2001.[43] In 2005, Assistant FBI director Chris Swecker told Congress that "gangs from California, particularly in the Los Angeles area, have a major influence on Mexican-Americans and Central American gangs in this country and in Latin America. . . . The Mara Salvatrucha gang, or MS-13, is a violent gang composed primarily of Central American immigrants which originated in Los Angeles and has now spread across the country. MS-13 gang members are primarily from El Salvador, Honduras, and Guatemala . . . [They] now have a presence in more than 31 states and the District of Columbia.[44]

In 2005, the Government Accountability Office reported that

"at the federal level, the number of criminal aliens incarcerated increased from about 42,000 at the end of calendar year 2001 to about 49,000 at the end of calendar year 2004—a 15 percent increase. The percentage of all federal prisoners who are criminal aliens has remained the same over the last three years—about 27 percent. The majority of criminal aliens incarcerated at the end of calendar year 2004 were identified as citizens of Mexico." At the state level, "the 50 states received [partial] reimbursement for incarcerating about 77,000 criminal aliens in fiscal year 2002. . . . At the local level, . . . [i]n fiscal year 2003 [the federal government partially] reimbursed about 700 local governments for [incarcerating] about 147,000 criminal aliens."[45] "Some state and local governments have expressed concerns about the impact that criminal aliens have on already overcrowded prisons and jails and that the federal government reimburses them for only a portion of their costs for incarcerating criminal aliens."[46]

Health costs and risks are also growing throughout the nation. The late Madeleine Pelner Cosman wrote, "By default, we grant health passes to illegal aliens. Yet many illegal aliens harbor fatal diseases that American medicine fought and vanquished long ago, such as drug-resistant tuberculosis, malaria, leprosy, plague, polio, dengue, and Chagas disease."[47]

Cosman noted, "The Emergency Medical Treatment and Active Labor Act (EMTALA) requires every emergency department (ED) to treat anyone who enters with an 'emergency,' including cough, headache, hangnail, cardiac arrest, herniated lumbar disc, drug addition, alcohol overdose, gunshot wound, automobile trauma, human immunodeficiency virus (HIV)–positive infection, mental problem, or personality disorder. The definition of emergency is flexible and vague enough to include almost any condition. Any patient coming to a hospital ED requesting 'emergency' care must be screened and treated until ready for discharge, or stabilized for transfer—whether or not insured, 'documented,' or able to pay. A woman in labor must remain to deliver her child."[48] "High-technology EDs have degenerated into free medical offices. Between 1993 and 2003, 60 California hospitals closed because half their services became unpaid. Another 24 California hospitals verge on closure. Even ambulances from Mexico come to American EDs with indigents because the drivers know that EMTALA requires accepting patients who come *within 250 yards of a hospital*. That geographic limit has figured in many lawsuits."[49]

These costs are obviously extremely burdensome to hospitals and physicians. They are either passed on to patients who have insurance or the hospitals and physicians must absorb them. Moreover, the threat of reemerging diseases is real and serious.

Making matters worse is the government of Mexico. Columbia University professor Claudio Lomnitz argues that in Mexico "corruption has also played a central role in conserving privilege, in keeping competitors out of specific markets, in creating an organized labor sector that stands apart from other sectors of the working class and in conserving the prerogatives of lineage."[50] Furthermore, the economic model of centralized socialism has led to widespread disparities in income. It is, therefore, the goal of Mexican authorities to export to the United States the foot soldiers of potential revolution to preserve their society's culture of corruption and privilege.

One of the ways in which this is accomplished is by the Mexican government promoting the idea of *extraterritorial nationalism* among its citizens—that is, the notion that Mexican citizens have an indigenous claim to large swaths of the United States. On July 23, 1997, Mexican president Ernesto Zedillo declared that "I have proudly affirmed that the Mexican nation extends beyond the territory enclosed by its borders [the southwestern United States] and that Mexican migrants are an important—a very important—part of it."[51] This attitude is not confined to Mexican leadership, but rather is shared by the country at large. According to a 2002 survey conducted by Zogby International, 58 percent of Mexicans agree with the statement "The territory of the United States' southwest rightfully belongs to Mexico."[52]

And the Mexican government is not leaving anything to chance. It is aggressively interfering with the internal affairs of the United States. As Heather Mac Donald writes, "Mexican leaders have . . . tasked their nation's U.S. consulates with spreading Mexican culture into American schools and communities."[53] There are forty-seven Mexican consulates in the United States. They publish guides advising their citizens on ways to illegally enter the United States and avoid detection. They help hire lawyers and coordinate with Mexican-American groups to assist illegal immigrants in the United States. They issue [matricula] consular cards "as a way for illegals to obtain privileges that the U.S. usually reserves for legal residents. The consulates started aggressively lobbying American governmental officials and banks to accept matriculas as valid IDs for driver's licenses, checking accounts, mortgage lending, and other benefits. The only type of Mexican who would need such identification is an illegal one; legal aliens already have sufficient documentation to get driver's licenses or bank accounts. . . ."[54]

Mac Donald adds, "Since 1990, Mexico has embarked on a series of initiatives to import Mexican culture into the U.S. Mexico's five-year development plan in 1995 announced that the 'Mexican nation extends . . . its border'—into the United States. Accordingly, the government would 'strengthen solidarity programs with the Mexican communities abroad by emphasizing their Mexican roots, and supporting literacy programs in Spanish and teaching of the history, values, and traditions of our country.' "[55] It seems the Mexican population in the United States has gotten the message. In 2001, just 34 percent of eligible Mexicans became citizens, compared with 58 percent of other Latin Americans, 65 percent of Canadians and Europeans, and 67 percent of Asians.[56]

What is the Conservative to make of all this?

The evidence of the civil society's degradation cannot be ignored. A confluence of government policies, both long-standing and more recent, is transforming the nation in ways that threaten its survival. The Statist, of course, looks over the horizon and sees opportunity. The demographic changes he is importing and protecting empower him. The poor and uneducated enhance the Statist's electoral and welfare-state constituency.

The Statist finds common ground with the neo-Statist, which is best exemplified by this statement by former Republican vice presidential candidate Jack Kemp: "We are going to make sure that America is open to legal immigration because that is the wealth and the talent and the entrepreneurial skills for the 21st Century."[57] Of course, if legal immigration emphasized wealth, talent, and entrepreneurial skills, American society would be the better for it. Instead, it emphasizes birthright citizenship and chain migration and encourages illegal immigration, which have led to the current state of immigration anarchy.

Alexander Hamilton wrote that the well-being of society depends "essentially on the energy of a common national sentiment, on a uniformity of principles and habits, on the exemption of the citizens from foreign bias and prejudice, and on that love of country which will almost invariably be found to be closely connected with birth, education and family."[58] He added, "In the composition of society, the harmony of the ingredients is all-important, and whatever tends to a discordant intermixture must have an injurious tendency."[59]

For the Conservative, to say that America is a nation of immigrants and no more is to conflate society with immigration and treat them as equivalents. They are not. Immigration can contribute to the well-being of society, but it can also contribute to its demise. The social contract is a compact between and among Americans, not Americans and the world's citizens. The American government governs by the consent of its citizens, not the consent of aliens and their governments. Moreover, American citizens are not interchangeable with all other citizens, American culture is not interchangeable with all other cultures, and the American government is not interchangeable with all other governments. The purpose of immigration policies must be to preserve and improve the American society.

It is all the more astounding, therefore, that the Statist and neo-Statist nearly succeeded in radically and permanently altering "the harmony of the ingredients" in American society when, in 2006, they proposed a so-called Comprehensive Immigration Reform Act (CIRA), which, according to the Heritage Foundation, would have not only granted amnesty to millions of illegal aliens, but would have allowed an estimated 103 million legal aliens to migrate to the United States over twenty years.[60] How? The huge increase in the number of legal aliens and the grant of amnesty to illegal aliens, layered on top of chain migration and birthright citizenship, would have drastically and quickly increased the number of new legal immigrants and the nation's overall population. Moreover, future efforts to limit immigration would have been extremely difficult because of the enormous electoral clout such a significant and largely unassimilated ethnic population would exercise. But CIRA's defeat is likely temporary, since President Obama promises to sign it, or something like it, should it reach his desk.

The Statist has been accustomed to setting immigration policy without notice from the American people. But the people are now witnesses to the events and costs associated with the current state of immigration in their own communities. They have made clear they want some order brought to the chaos. The evidence and prudence guide the Conservative's priorities, which include securing the borders to prevent not only illegal aliens from crossing into the United States, but criminals and terrorists as well; enforcing current immigration laws, including fining and prosecuting businesses that hire illegal aliens, deporting newly apprehended illegal aliens, and deporting aliens who overstay their visas; denying sanctuary cities federal funds for contributing to lawless behavior; English and assimilation promoted in all the nation's institutions, not bilingualism and multiculturalism; limits on the number of aliens admitted into the country, to allow for workable assimilation; the denial of most social services to illegal aliens to deter their migration to the United States; repelling Mexico's interference in the internal affairs of the nation; and the elimination of chain migration and birthright citizenship, which put the alien's desires before society's well-being.

As is his practice, the Statist engages in tactics intended to proscribe debate. Those who dissent from his immigration policies are often characterized as exclusionists, nativists, xenophobes, or even racists. The neo-Statist offers no alternative to the status quo and condemns the Conservative for not going along. He not only accommodates Balkanization but panders to it. But the good citizen contributes to the social cohesion of the civil society—for his own benefit and the benefit of that society. And he expects his government to do the same. The Conservative believes that to the extent immigration can be applied to that purpose, it is desirable. When it is not, it is destructive of those ends.

10

ON SELF-PRESERVATION

THE CONSERVATIVE BELIEVES THAT the moral imperative of all public policy must be the preservation and improvement of American society. Similarly, the object of American foreign policy must be no different.

The Founders recognized that America had to be strong politically, economically, culturally, and militarily to survive and thrive in a complex, ever-changing global environment not only in their time but for all time. History bears this out. After the Revolutionary War, the Founders realized that the Confederation was inadequate to conduct foreign affairs, since each state was free to act on its own. There could be no coherent national security policy, because there was no standing army and each state ultimately was responsible for its own defense. The nation's economy was vulnerable to pirates who were terrorizing transatlantic shipping routes and thereby inhibiting trade and commerce. And the British and Spanish empires were looming threats.

The authority of the national government to raise and maintain a standing army and use military power within the framework of a republican system was among the first matters addressed by the Framers when they presented the finished Constitution to the states for ratification. After reviewing a litany of European interests and conflicts in North America, John Jay in "Federalist 4" wrote, "The people of America are aware that inducements to war may arise out of these circumstances, as well as from others not so obvious at present, and that whenever such inducements may find fit time and opportunity for operation, pretenses to color and justify them will not be wanting. Wisely, therefore, do they consider union and a good national government as necessary to put and keep them in such a situation as, instead of inviting war, will tend to repress and discourage it. The situation consists in the best possible state of defense, and necessarily depends on the government, the arms, and the resources of the country."[1] Indeed, one of the stated purposes of the Constitution is "to provide for the common defence."[2]

The Framers understood the complementary purposes of domestic and foreign policy. George Washington's Farewell Address of 1796 is often misunderstood as a proclamation of isolationism. This ignores its historical context. At the time, Washington was concerned with the very survival of the young nation. The address is a call for prudence—not only in dealings and relationships with foreign states, but in issues that threaten national unity.

In his address, Washington warned against the influences of popular passions on establishing permanent and overarching allegiances to, or prejudices against, any foreign power. He issued his warning because the American public was deeply divided in its sentiments relating to the European powers that were at war. The nascent political parties, the Federalists and the Anti-Federalists (or Democratic-Republicans), were coalescing around support for different countries—the Federalists for Britain, the Anti-Federalists for France. Throughout his presidency, Washington tried to steer a course of strict neutrality between the two countries while promoting commercial relationships and vigorous trade with both sides in the conflict.[3] The address makes clear he did so not because neutrality was an end in itself, but because he feared that taking sides could split the country apart.[4]

Washington also believed that the nation's survival required a strong national defense. In his first annual message to Congress, on January 8, 1790, barely eight months after taking office, Washington said, "Among the many interesting objects which will engage your attention, that of providing for the common defense will merit particular regard. To be prepared for war is one of the most effectual means of preserving peace."[5] In his fifth annual message, on December 3, 1793, Washington offered a stronger, more substantial elaboration of this principle: "There is a rank due to the United States among nations which will be withheld, if not absolutely lost, by the reputation of weakness. If we desire to avoid insult, we must be able to repel it; if we desire to secure peace, one of the most powerful instruments of our rising prosperity, it must be known that we are at all times ready for war."[6]

But few knew better than Washington that America must establish alliances that have as their purpose the protection and well-being of the nation. Without the crucial material aid and military support of France (and other nations), the decisive Battle of Yorktown and perhaps the Revolutionary War itself might have been lost. Washington was neither an isolationist nor an interventionist. Yes, Washington was skeptical of alliances, but when in America's best interests, he made them. Washington preferred diplomacy to war, but he knew war was sometimes unavoidable. By word and deed, as general, president, and statesman, Washington spent his public life pursuing the preservation and improvement of American society. Washington's example is thus flexibility in means to achieve the immutable end: national security.

Agreeing with Washington, Claremont Institute senior fellow and University of Dallas professor Thomas West writes, "For the Founders, foreign and domestic policy were supposed to serve the same end: the security of the people in their person and property. Therefore, foreign policy was conceived primarily as defensive. Foreign attack was to be deterred by having strong arms or repulsed by force. Alliances were to be entered into with the understanding that a self-governing nation must keep itself aloof from the quarrels of other nations, except as needed for national defense. Government had no right to spend the taxes or lives of its own citizens to spread democracy to other nations or to engage in enterprises aiming at imperialistic hegemony."[7]

West would also agree, however, that a defensive foreign policy does not exclude the necessity of preemptive action. In 1787, James Wilson, a prominent Founder, rejected the argument that America had to wait until attacked to exercise military power and mocked the proponents of this notion: "Whatever may be the provocation, however important the object in view, and however necessary dispatch and secrecy may be, still the declaration must precede the preparation, and the enemy will be informed of your intentions, not only before you are equipped for an attack, but even before you are fortified for a defense. The consequence is too obvious to require any further delineation."[8] Of course, there are occasions when America has suffered grievously, including on 9/11, for failing to act preemptively. Moreover, in the age of rogue regimes pursuing nuclear weapons, there clearly are occasions when preemption is prudent. For a government to be irresolute in the face of a growing or imminent threat to its citizenry is suicidal.

What of the notion of spreading democracy to other nations, which in one form or another appears to be part of the strategy of recent administrations of both political parties?

In 2005, columnist George Will put the question to William F. Buckley, Jr., asking about the war in Iraq.

WILL: Today, we have a very different kind of foreign policy. . . . And the premise of the Bush Doctrine is that America must spread democracy because our national security depends upon it. And America can spread democracy. It knows how. It can engage in nation building. This is conservative or not?

BUCKLEY: It's not at all conservative. It's anything but conservative. It's not conservative at all inasmuch as conservatism doesn't invite unnecessary challenges. It insists on coming to terms with the world as it is, and the notion that merely by affirming these high ideals we can affect highly entrenched systems.

WILL: But something odd is happening in conservatism. And we have a president [George W. Bush] and an administration that clearly is conservative, accepted as that, yet it is nation-building

in the Middle East. And conservatism seems to be saying govern‑
ment can't run Amtrak but it can run the Middle East. . . .

BUCKLEY: The ambition of conservatism . . . properly extends
to saying [that] where there are no human rights, it's not a society
I can truly respect. It's impossible to draw up a template that gives
us an orderly sense of "send democracy there," but let this go for a
while. One recognizes that you can't export democracy every‑
where simultaneously.[9]

Certainly America cannot export democracy everywhere si‑
multaneously, nor should it attempt to. For one thing, it is im‑
practical. There are cultures and regimes that are not receptive to
such overtures. Furthermore, the loss of American lives and the
enormous financial costs in chasing such unrealistic ends would
threaten the preservation and improvement of American society.
It would demoralize the population and desensitize it to real
threats that endanger the society.

However, there are occasions when democracy building is pru‑
dent. The European Recovery Program, better known as the Mar‑
shall Plan of 1948, had among its purposes the promotion and
preservation of democracy through the provision of billions of
dollars in economic and military aid to several European nations
defeated in World War II. Among other things, it would and did
help repel the spread of Soviet communism through what re‑
mained of free Europe, which was clearly in America's interests.
More recently, while democracy may not take hold in Afghani‑
stan for the long term, it is still a perfectly sound objective, given
the vacuum that was filled by the Taliban and al‑Qaeda in the
aftermath of the Soviet Union's defeat in that country and

America's subsequent disassociation. The key is that these decisions must never be motivated by utopianism or imperialism but by actual circumstances requiring the defense of America against real threats.

As for Iraq, the Will-Buckley exchange suggests their opposition to the war was a larger criticism of a perceived doctrine requiring the imposition of democracy worldwide—although Will has also called Iraq a "war of choice."[10] America has engaged in wars of choice in the past, including during the nineteenth century, when, under the banner of Manifest Destiny, the United States government increased American territory by military threat and force to include the Southwest, West, and Pacific Northwest. The expansion of the nation's contiguous borders has undoubtedly improved American society. While America may have felt threatened from Britain, Mexico, and other countries that controlled these territories, the fact is that the nation was intent on expansion.

If the war in Iraq is understood as an effort to defeat a hostile regime that threatened both America's allies and interests in the region, the war and the subsequent attempt at democratic governance in that country can be justified as consistent with founding and conservative principles. Indeed, since the Will-Buckley exchange, when victory in Iraq appeared elusive to some, changes in military and political strategies dramatically improved the situation. Of course, Iraq is not necessarily a model for future engagements but nor can it be easily dismissed as unreasonable and imprudent. Saddam's Iraq had a history of aggressive behavior against America's ally Kuwait (and threatened Saudi Arabia) and had actively pursued nuclear weapons (such as Iraq's Osirak nuclear reactor, destroyed by Israel in 1981). The United States and its allies no longer face the prospect of a nuclear Iraq under the control of a megalomaniac. For now, at least, it is one less destabilizing threat to American interests.

Conversely, America has, will, and must make alliances with nondemocratic regimes and even former enemies if, under the right circumstances, doing so preserves and improves American society. During World War II, the United States allied with the Soviet Union in order to defeat the Axis powers, including Nazi Germany. The Soviet Union under Joseph Stalin was a genocidal, imperialistic regime. But America's survival was at stake. And, in fact, the alliance did preserve the nation. Subsequent to World War II, the Soviet Union was America's greatest threat. When President Jimmy Carter based his foreign policy on advancing human rights worldwide, it not only led to Soviet expansionism in Afghanistan, Africa, and Latin America, but also toppled the Shah of Iran—a longtime American ally—and catalyzed the Islamic fundamentalist movement throughout the Middle East. Today the Soviet Union does not exist (although Russia remains a threat) but the Islamic regime in Iran is on the verge of acquiring nuclear weapons and is the single most destabilizing force in the Middle East. The doctrinal rather than prudential promotion of "democracy" or "human rights," as practiced by Carter, can be destructive of America's best interests.

The Conservative believes that unalienable rights attach to all human beings, but it is not necessarily the responsibility of the United States to enforce those rights. How can it be? However, he also believes that there are times when evil perpetrated by a regime is so horrific that to ignore it tears at the moral core of

American civil society. Although there can be no single doctrine that defines the elements of action or inaction in every case, once again prudence must dictate if and when the cost of American lives and treasure is worth intervention on these grounds.

The Conservative does not seek rigid adherence to any specific course of action: neutrality or alliance, preemptive war or defensive posture, nation building or limited military strike. The benchmark, again, is whether any specific path will serve the nation's best interests. It is difficult to imagine a theory under which a society could otherwise survive. Indeed, the Monroe Doctrine of 1823 and its various iterations since stand today for the proposition that the United States will not tolerate threats against its survival, whether in the Western Hemisphere or anywhere in the world.

For the Statist, however, U.S. foreign policy is another opportunity to enhance his own authority at the expense of the civil society. In 2007, then-senator Barack Obama set forth his views to the Chicago Council on Global Affairs:

> In today's globalized world, the security of the American people is inextricably linked to the security of all people. When narco-trafficking and corruption threaten democracy in Latin America, it's America's problem too. When poor villagers in Indonesia have no choice but to send chickens to market infected with avian flu, it cannot be seen as a distant concern. When religious schools in Pakistan teach hatred to young children, our children are threatened as well.
>
> Whether it's global terrorism or pandemic disease, dramatic climate change or the proliferation of weapons of mass annihila-

tion, the threats we face at the dawn of the 21st century can no longer be contained by borders and boundaries. . . .

And America must lead by reaching out to all those living disconnected lives of despair in the world's forgotten corners— because while there will always be those who succumb to hate and strap bombs to their bodies, there are millions more who want to take another path—who want our beacon of hope to shine its light their way. . . .

[Another way] America will lead again is to invest in our common humanity—to ensure that those who live in fear and want today can live with dignity and opportunity tomorrow.

We have heard much over the last six years about how America's larger purpose in the world is to promote the spread of freedom—that it is the yearning of all who live in the shadow of tyranny and despair.

I agree. But this yearning is not satisfied by simply deposing a dictator and setting up a ballot box. The true desire of all mankind is not only to live free lives, but lives marked by dignity and opportunity; by security and simple justice.

Delivering on these universal aspirations requires basic sustenance like food and clean water; medicine and shelter. It also requires a society that is supported by the pillars of a sustainable democracy—a strong legislature, an independent judiciary, the rule of law, a vibrant civil society, a free press, and an honest police force. It requires building the capacity of the world's weakest states and providing them what they need to reduce poverty, build healthy and educated communities, develop markets, and generate wealth. And it requires states that have the capacity to fight terrorism, halt the proliferation of deadly weap-

ons, and build the health care infrastructure needed to prevent
and treat such deadly diseases as HIV/AIDS and malaria. . . .

But if the next President can restore the American people's
trust—if they know that he or she is acting with their best inter-
ests at heart, with prudence and wisdom and some measure of
humility—then I believe the American people will be ready to
see America lead again.[11]

Several elements of Obama's global vision must be addressed.
When he says, *"The security of the American people is inextricably*
linked to the security of all people," what is meant by "security of all
people" of the world? How, in every case, is America's security
related to their security? It clearly is not. And if a regime refuses
to secure for its people that which America believes it should,
what then? Moreover, are there not times when the security of
other people conflicts with the security of America?

"And America must lead by reaching out to all those living discon-
nected lives of despair in the world's forgotten corners."

What does it mean to live a disconnected life of despair? If
included among the disconnected, for example, are the millions
of starving people living under the iron fist of North Korean communism, how do Americans reach out to them? But "disconnected
lives of despair" appears to mean much more than the denial of
liberty to people in the forgotten corners of the world. It is a mes-
sianic attitude that has no basis in reality.

"[Another way] America will lead again is to invest in our common
humanity—to ensure that those who live in fear and want today can
live with dignity and opportunity tomorrow."

America will invest what and where? And how can America ensure that people in, say, Zimbabwe and scores of other places can live with dignity and opportunity? And does such a purpose and mission exclude Iraq, where Saddam Hussein was terrorizing and brutalizing large segments of the Iraqi population? And if not, why not?

"Delivering on these universal aspirations requires basic sustenance like food and clean water; medicine and shelter. It also requires a society that is supported by the pillars of a sustainable democracy—a strong legislature, an independent judiciary, the rule of law, a vibrant civil society, a free press, and an honest police force. It requires building the capacity of the world's weakest states and providing them what they need to reduce poverty, build healthy and educated communities, develop markets, and generate wealth."

And how are these things to be accomplished? No insight is provided into the myriad of complicated and complex obstacles—both within the United States and in other countries—that would have to be overcome, because they are too numerous to make tangible and too onerous to accomplish. Moreover, if the government were to compel Americans to give of their labor, treasure, and lives to chase the unachievable—an imagined global civil society—America could not survive or improve upon itself.

"But if the next President can restore the American people's trust— if they know that he or she is acting with their best interests at heart, with prudence and wisdom and some measure of humility—then I believe the American people will be ready to see America lead again."

How would this restore the American people's trust, and in

whom and what? How is committing them to a staggeringly unrealistic global task acting in their best interests? Where is the
prudence and wisdom in such a reckless overstatement of human
possibilities, which completely ignores history and man's experience?

In truth, the Statist is and will be no more successful in his
foreign policy promises than in his domestic promises. International utopianism has no better chance than its domestic brand.

But for all his talk of America changing the world, the Statist
speaks not of American sovereignity but "global citizenship."[12]
He speaks not of America as a nation-state but as one nation
among many. Rather than maintain its superpower status and act
in its own best interests, the United States should relinquish its
hard-earned position in favor of multilateral power sharing and
conduct foreign policy—including decisions about military action in its own defense—through coalitions and international
organizations. In this way, America's interests are subsumed and
contained by the supposed interests of the whole. And the rest of
the world will look approvingly upon the United States for empowering other countries to participate in decisions about
America's survival.

The Statist seeks treaties not to preserve and improve American society, but to commit the United States to a course of
conduct that cannot be easily reversed with the change of administrations. He will enter into treaties that include the Convention
on the Rights of the Child (signed in 1995 but not ratified due to
sovereignty and other concerns); the Convention on All Forms
of Discrimination Against Women (which the Senate has refused
to ratify since President Carter signed it in 1980); the Compre-

hensive Test Ban Treaty (signed by Clinton in 1996, rejected by the Senate in 1999); the Kyoto Protocol on climate change (signed by Clinton in 1998 but never ratified; Bush withdrew it in 2001);[13] the Convention on the Law of the Sea (which would restrict U.S. commercial and military operations, but the Senate has not taken it up); and the International Criminal Court (which the United States has not joined). In each instance, decisions will be made through international bureaucracies that do not have as their moral imperative the preservation and improvement of American society. This is a dangerous gambit.

America's adversaries and enemies do not consider themselves global citizens. Nor are they constrained by international sensibilities and arrangements. A resurgent Russia, an aggressive China, communist movements growing in Latin America, rogue regimes in North Korea and Iran, Islamic terrorism, to name a few, all reject the Statist's Utopia as a weakness to be exploited. They are not motivated by world opinion but by their own desires. They seek strategic—economic and military—advantage. For example, while China locks up oil contracts with countries in Africa and Latin America and Russia lays claim to the North Pole to expand its access to crude oil, the Statist asserts that America is only "5 percent of the world's population, [but] consumes one quarter of the world's total energy supply,"[14] suggesting that America must become poorer so the rest of the world might become richer. The Statist believes Americans are gluttonous and wasteful, taking from the world that which belongs to others, whereas the Conservative believes Americans are successful and productive, contributing to their own preservation and improvement. The United States also produces and supplies goods and services to the rest of the world, thereby improving their lot. Furthermore, many other countries are incapable of accessing or utilizing natural resources as a result of their own governments, cultures, and societies.

Despite the Statist's lofty talk of global citizenship, in practice he protects if not augments his domestic position. Therefore, he opposes free trade, because it would alienate his union constituency, which sees protectionism as job security. He opposes the use of DDT to eradicate diseases in the most impoverished areas of the world, to appease his environmental acolytes, for whom DDT is a cause célèbre. The Statist will guard from the international community factions within American society that he considers essential to his authority. The Conservative, on the other hand, will restrict or prevent the provision of certain technologies and military know-how to hostile regimes (through such mechanisms as export controls), thereby limiting free trade with such regimes, not to benefit a favored constituency or enhance his own authority but to preserve America's security—which, in turn, preserves free trade generally. Once again, the Statist is motivated to accumulate and maintain his authority, whereas the Conservative is motivated to preserve and improve the civil society.

The Statist also uses the idea of global citizenship to denigrate the effectiveness of war efforts that he does not lead and agitate the public against his political opponents. Indeed, the Statist adopts the language and tactics of America's adversaries in criticizing American foreign and national security policies. For example, in the war on terrorism, the United States has been accused by various countries, self-described human rights groups, international bureaucrats, among others, of using torture in the interrogation and detention of al-Qaeda terrorists. These critics have attacked critically important, albeit rarely used, methodologies for securing intelligence and neutralizing the enemy as violations of terrorists' human rights—including waterboarding, which simulates drowning. The technique has now been banned, but was used on only three terrorists—Khalid Sheik Mohammed, the mastermind of 9/11, Abu Zubaydah, Osama bin Laden's chief of operations, and Abd al-Rahim al-Nashiri, who the government says coordinated the attack on the USS *Cole*. The technique reportedly led to securing important information that prevented dozens of planned al-Qaeda attacks.[15] The Statist has succeeded in characterizing something as torture that is not torture, for the purpose of banning even its judicious use. How is banning waterboarding—which Barack Obama did among his first acts as president—morally defensible when a few minutes of simulated drowning applied against the operational leader of 9/11 reportedly saved an untold number of innocent American lives?

Even the detention of al-Qaeda terrorists at Guantánamo Bay, Cuba, under the watchful eyes of the media, antiwar groups, defense lawyers, and statist politicians who have toured the detention center over a period of years has been made controversial. Obama also issued an executive order that will close the facility within a year of his taking office. And the insistence on treating the detained terrorists as soldiers under international law (the Geneva Conventions),[16] which specifically excludes them from such a designation since they are waging war illegally, and also treating them as quasi-American citizens for the purpose of applying constitutional-like due process standards in determining their fate, flies in the face of legal and historical precedent. How does American society benefit from these approaches? Terrorists, the earliest of whom were pirates, have never been considered equivalent to regular armed forces by any president up to now. Granting new rights to terrorists, which makes their barbarism more difficult to stop and their schemes more difficult to uncover, is not morally defensible.

While empowering the terrorist with new rights, thereby increasing the threat against Americans, the Statist claims violations of Americans' civil liberties with the passage of the post-9/11 Patriot Act. As former terrorist prosecutor Andrew McCarthy has explained, the act "removes obstacles that have for years prevented the law-enforcement and counterintelligence sides of the government from pooling information to confront the terrorist threat. [And] it ushers several long-established investigative techniques into the era of 21st-century technology, bringing them to bear on terrorism with the same effectiveness they have long exhibited in rooting out far-less-heinous crimes, such as drug trafficking and health-care fraud." The law provides for judicial review at every important stage as well.[17] The Statist also has opposed the interception of enemy communications, such as email and cell phone contacts, without approval from a court. But his position is contrary to all legal precedent, historical practice, and highly impractical, given the speed by which such communications occur. Yet again he claims the practice threatens Americans' civil liberties. Where is the *actual* evidence of widespread civil liberties' abuses against American citizens? It is nonexistent.

The war against terrorism requires infiltration, interception, detention, and interrogation, all of which are aimed at *preventing* another catastrophic attack against American citizens within the United States and American soldiers on the battlefield. The post-9/11 mix of laws and policies instituted by President George W. Bush, which are intended to protect American society from mortal threats, did, in fact, succeed in securing the American people's unalienable rights within the framework of the Constitution. The Statist knows this, but he is intolerant of the successful leadership of others, for it delays his own ascendancy. He must denigrate those who obstruct him. And once in power, his threshold for actual civil liberties violations is often lowered.

During World War II, Franklin Roosevelt ordered the unconstitutional internment of 110,000 Japanese-Americans, which was upheld by an activist Supreme Court.[18] Roosevelt remains among the Statist's most adored leaders and the Court among his most venerated institutions. When Robert Kennedy served as attorney general of the United States in the 1960s, he did nothing to stop the illegal bugging of Martin Luther King, Jr.'s telephone by the FBI.[19] Today, the federal Justice Department building is named after Kennedy. Under President Bill Clinton, the National Security Agency launched the Echelon surveillance program, in which the U.S. government routinely intercepts international email, telephone, and fax communications of citizen and terrorist alike.[20] It drew virtually no attention from self-identified civil libertarian groups.

For the Conservative, there is no doubt that the relentless efforts of the Statist to criminalize war—by dragging strategic and operational decisions into the courtroom, where inexpert judicial activists second-guess an elected president and his military and intelligence experts—will make securing the nation against future attacks far more difficult. The extent to which the Statist is willing to expose the nation to known external threats during wartime demonstrates the zealotry with which he now pursues his ambitions.

EPILOGUE

A CONSERVATIVE MANIFESTO

So DISTANT IS AMERICA today from its founding principles that it is difficult to precisely describe the nature of American government. It is not strictly a constitutional republic, because the Constitution has been and continues to be easily altered by a judicial oligarchy that mostly enforces, if not expands, the Statist's agenda. It is not strictly a representative republic, because so many edicts are produced by a maze of administrative departments that are unknown to the public and detached from its sentiment. It is not strictly a federal republic, because the states that gave the central government life now live at its behest. What, then, is it? It is a society steadily transitioning toward statism. If the Conservative does not come to grips with the significance of this transformation, he will be devoured by it.

The Republican Party acts as if it is without recourse. Republican administrations—with the exception of a brief eight-year respite under Ronald Reagan—more or less remain on the glide path set by Franklin Roosevelt and the New Deal. The latest and most stunning example is the trillions of dollars in various bailout schemes that President George W. Bush oversaw in the last months of his administration. When asked about it, he made this remarkable statement: "I've abandoned free-market principles to save the free-market system."[1]

And he did more than that. In approving the expenditure of $17.4 billion in loans to General Motors and Chrysler, President Bush overrode Congress, which had rejected the plan, and in doing so violated the Constitution's separation of powers doctrine. Just as another Republican president, Herbert Hoover, laid the foundation for Franklin Roosevelt's New Deal, Bush has, in words and actions, done the same for President Barack Obama—the most ideologically pure Statist and committed counterrevolutionary to occupy the Oval Office.

Republicans seem clueless on how to slow, contain, and reverse the Statist's agenda. They seem to fear returning to first principles, lest they be rejected by the electorate, and so prefer to tinker ineffectively and timidly on the edges. As such, are they not abandoning what they claim to support? If the bulk of the people reject the civil society for the Statist's Utopia, preferring subjugation to citizenship, then the end is near anyway. But even in winning an election, governing without advancing first principles is a hollow victory indeed. Its imprudence is self-evident. This is not the way of the Conservative; it is the way of the neo-Statist—subservient to a "reality" created by the Statist rather than the reality of unalienable rights granted by the Creator.

So, what can be done? I do not pretend to have all the answers. Moreover, the act of writing a book places practical limits on what can be said at a given time. However, I do have some thoughts.

The Conservative must become more engaged in public matters. It is in his nature to live and let live, to attend to his family, to volunteer time with his church and synagogue, and to quietly assist a friend, a neighbor, or even a stranger. These are certainly admirable qualities that contribute to the overall health of the community. But it is no longer enough. The Statist's counterrevolution has turned the instrumentalities of public affairs and public governance against the civil society. They can no longer be left to the devices of the Statist, which is largely the case today.

This will require a new generation of conservative activists, larger in number, shrewder, and more articulate than before, who seek to blunt the Statist's counterrevolution—not imitate it—and gradually and steadily reverse course. More conservatives than before will need to seek elective and appointed office, fill the ranks of the administrative state, hold teaching positions in public schools and universities, and find positions in Hollywood and the media where they can make a difference in infinite ways. The Statist does not have a birthright ownership to these institutions. The Conservative must fight for them, mold them, and where appropriate, eliminate them where they are destructive to the preservation and improvement of the civil society.

Parents and grandparents must take it upon themselves to teach their children and grandchildren to believe in and appreciate the principles of the American civil society and stress the import of preserving and improving the society. They will need to teach their offspring that the Statist threatens their generation's liberty and prosperity, and to resist ideologically alluring trends and fads. Parents and grandparents by the millions can counteract the Statist's indoctrination of their children and grandchildren in government schools and by other Statist institutions simply by conferring their knowledge, beliefs, and ideals on them over the dinner table, in the car, or at bedtime. If undertaken on an intimate, purposeful, and consistent basis, it will shape a generation of new conservatives.

And education should not stop at the front door. We, the people, are a vast army of educators and communicators. When the occasion arises in conversations with neighbors, friends, coworkers and others, take the time to explain conservative principles and their value to the individual, family, and society generally.

The Conservative should acquire knowledge outside the Statist's universe. He should not ignore the media, Hollywood, government schools, and universities, but they should not be the primary sources of information that shape the Conservative's worldview. Technology has made access easy to an unprecedented wealth of resources that contribute to the Conservative's understanding, including the Avalon Project,[2] which makes available online, among other things, a large collection of the nation's founding documents; the Atlas Economic Research Foundation,[3] which offers sources of free-market thinking; the CATO Institute, which produces scholarly materials oriented around Adam Smith's philosophy; and the Heritage Foundation, which produces scholarly materials oriented around Edmund Burke. Moreover, established publications, such as *Human Events* and *National Review*, engage in conservative thought relating to current news events. Talk radio provides a dynamic forum for conservative thought and debate. There are academic institutions, particularly

Hillsdale College and Chapman University, that provide formal educational opportunities. Groups such as Young America's Foundation, the Intercollegiate Studies Institute, and the Leadership Institute promote conservatism on college campuses throughout the nation. There are, in fact, many outstanding conservative organizations and institutions, too numerous to list, that are accessible to the public.

The Statist has also become masterful at controlling the public vocabulary. For example, when challenged on global warming, he accuses the skeptic of being a "denier," "favoring corporate polluters," or being "against saving the planet." Draconian measures that threaten liberty and prosperity, such as cap-and-trade, are marketed in appealing and benign slogans, such as "going green." The Statist never destroys, he "reforms." He never disenfranchises, he "empowers."

President Ronald Reagan understood the power of words. He framed the debate on his terms.

> How can limited government and fiscal restraint be equated with lack of compassion for the poor? How can a tax break that puts a little more money in the weekly paychecks of working people be seen as an attack on the needy? Since when do we in America believe that our society is made up of two diametrically opposed classes—one rich, one poor—both in a permanent state of conflict and neither able to get ahead except at the expense of the other? Since when do we in America accept this alien and discredited theory of social and class warfare? Since when do we in America endorse the politics of envy and division?[4]

Reagan dissected the Statist's language and recast the morality of the message. Americans are not at war with each other over money and class. And when Americans keep the fruits of their labor, it is a good thing. This is both seminal and fundamental. The Statist's vocabulary provides the Conservative with opportunities to highlight the Statist's duplicity and the bankruptcy of his ideas by stripping the rhetorical veneer from his message and contrasting it with the wisdom of the Conservative's principles. The battle over language, like the battle over ideas, is one that conservatives should relish.

The Statist has constructed a Rube Goldberg array of laws and policies that have institutionalized his objectives. His success breeds confidence in the limitlessness of his endeavors. For the Conservative, the challenge is daunting and the road will be long and hard. But it took the Statist nearly eighty years to get here, and it will take the Conservative at least as long to change the nation's direction. Still, there is no time to waste. The Conservative must act now. And in doing so he must reject the ideological boundaries the Statist and neo-Statist seek to impose on him, since they are self-defeating. He must be resolute in purpose yet flexible in approach. He must search out opportunities and exploit them. He must be both overt and covert. He must not reject compromise if the compromise is likely to advance the founding principles. He must reject compromise if the compromise is of little consequence and a diversionary end in itself.

The Conservative must take heart from, and learn the lessons of, his nation's history. America's founding, the Civil War, and World War II were epic and, at times, seemingly insurmountable wars of liberty against tyranny, which would have destroyed the civil society had they been lost. The challenge today is in many ways more complicated, because the "soft tyranny" comes from within and utilizes the nation's instrumentalities against itself. However, it is also a bloodless struggle and, therefore, should enlist all conservatives with the courage of their convictions.

There is a dynamic to prudential change that makes impossible the production of a step-by-step guide to tactical actions fixed for all circumstances and times. But tactical actions must be taken today, under known conditions, if the civil society is to survive tomorrow. Therefore, based on my own knowledge, observations, and experiences, herewith are some of the hard things the Conservative will have to do if the nation is to improve:

A CONSERVATIVE MANIFESTO

1. TAXATION

Eliminate the progressive income tax—replace it with a flat income tax or national sales tax—for its purpose is to redistribute wealth, not fund the constitutionally legitimate functions of the federal government.

All residents of the country must be required to pay the tax so they have a stake in limiting its abuse.

Eliminate the automatic withholding of taxes, for it conceals the extent to which the federal government is confiscating income from its citizens.

Eliminate the corporate income tax, for it is nothing more than double taxation on shareholders and consumers, and penalizes wealth and job creation.

Eliminate the death tax, for it denies citizens the right to confer the material value they have created during their lives to whomever they wish, including their family.

All federal income tax increases will require a supermajority vote of three-fifths of Congress.

Limit federal spending each year to less than 20 percent of the gross domestic product.[5]

2. ENVIRONMENT

Eliminate the special tax-exempt status granted to environmental groups, since they are not nonpartisan charitable foundations.

Eliminate special statutory authority granting environmental groups standing to bring lawsuits on behalf of the public, since their main purpose is to pursue the Statist's agenda through litigation.

Fight all efforts to use environmental regulations to set governmental industrial policies and diminish the nation's standard of living, such as "cap-and-trade" to regulate "man-made climate change."

3. JUDGES

Limit the Supreme Court's judicial-review power, which far exceeds the Framers' intent, by establishing a legislative veto over Court decisions—perhaps a two-thirds supermajority vote of both houses of Congress, not dissimilar from the congressional override authority of a presidential veto.

Eliminate lifetime tenure for federal judges, given the extra-

constitutional power they have amassed and their routine intervention in political and policy decisions—which the Constitution
leaves to the representative branches.

No judicial nominee should be confirmed who rejects the jurisprudence of originalism.

4. THE ADMINISTRATIVE STATE

Sunset all "independent" federal agencies each year, subject to
Congress affirmatively reestablishing them.

Require federal departments and agencies to reimburse individuals and enterprises for the costs associated with the devalua-
tion of their private property from the issuance of regulations that
compromise the use of their property.

Eliminate unions for federal government employees, since the
purpose of a civil service system is to promote merit and profes-
sionalism over patronage, and the purpose of federal unions is to
empower themselves and promote statism.

Reduce the civilian federal workforce by 20 percent or more.

5. GOVERNMENT EDUCATION

Eliminate monopoly control of government education by applying the antitrust laws to the National Education Association and
American Federation of Teachers; the monopoly is destructive of
quality education and competition and is unresponsive to the
taxpayers who fund it.

Eliminate tenure for government schoolteachers and college/

university professors, making them accountable for the quality of instruction they provide students.

Strip the statist agenda from curricula (such as multicultural-ism and global warming) and replace it with curricula that rein-force actual education and the preservation of the civil society through its core principles.

Eliminate the federal Department of Education, since educa-tion is primarily a state and local function.

6. IMMIGRATION

Eliminate chain migration, which grants control over immigra-tion policy to aliens and foreign governments, and which the Statist defends to expand his electoral and administrative state constituency.

Secure the nation's borders and discourage those who violate them—illegal alien and citizen lawbreaker alike—by enforcing the immigration laws.

End multiculturalism, diversity, and bilingualism in public in-stitutions, which beget poverty, animosity, and ethnic balkaniza-tion; promote assimilation and unity of citizenship, allegiance to American culture, and English as the official national language.

7. ENTITLEMENTS

Social Security is going bankrupt. Medicare is going bankrupt. Medicaid is going bankrupt. These programs and others have accumulated more than $50 trillion in IOUs due and payable by subsequent generations. Educate the young people about the intergenerational trap the Statist has laid for them—which will steal their liberty, labor, opportunities, and wealth—and build a future electoral force for whom the elixir of entitlements is understood as poisonous snake oil. These programs were created in politics and will have to be addressed in politics. Only in this way can they be contained, limited, and reformed.

Fight all efforts to nationalize the health-care system. National health care is the mother of all entitlement programs, for through it the Statist controls not only the material wealth of the individual but his physical well-being. Remind the people that politicians and bureaucrats, about whom they are already cynical, will ultimately have the final say over their choice of doctors, hospitals, and treatments—meaning the system will be politicized and bureaucratized. Remind them that this human experiment has been tried and has failed in places like Britain and Canada, where patients have been subjected to arbitrary treatment decisions, long waiting periods for lifesaving surgeries, antiquated medical technologies, the denial of high-cost pharmaceuticals available elsewhere, and the inefficient rationing of health care generally. And remind them that despite past utopian promises, the Statist rarely delivers.

8. FOREIGN POLICY AND SECURITY

Ensure that all foreign policy decisions are made for the purpose of preserving and improving American society.

Reject all treaties, entanglements, institutions, and enterprises that have as their purpose the supplantation of America's best interests, including its physical, cultural, economic, and military sovereignty, to an amorphous "global" interest.

Ensure that America remains the world's superpower. Ensure that at all times America's military forces are prepared for war to dissuade attacks, encourage peace, and, if necessary, win any war.

9. FAITH

Oppose all efforts to denude the nation of its founding justification—that is, God-given unalienable, natural rights that the government can neither confer on the individual nor deny to him. The Statist seeks the authority to do both, which explains his contempt for, or misuse of, faith. Moreover, faith provides the moral order that ties one generation to the next, and without which the civil society cannot survive.

10. THE CONSTITUTION

Demand that all public servants, elected or appointed, at all times uphold the Constitution and justify their public acts under the Constitution.

Oppose all efforts to "constitutionalize" the statist agenda.

Eliminate limits on and rationing of political free speech through unconstitutional "campaign finance" laws, which benefit incumbent politicians, the media, unions, and other Statist-related groups. Any American citizen or group of American citizens should be free to contribute to candidates as they wish, as long as the source, amount, and recipient of the contributions are made known.

Defeat all efforts to unconstitutionally regulate the content of political speech on broadcast outlets, such as radio. The Statist now seeks to consolidate the power he has accumulated by silencing noncompliant voices through a variety of schemes that would regulate broadcast content.

President Reagan said, "Freedom is never more than one generation away from extinction. We didn't pass it to our children in the bloodstream. It must be fought for, protected, and handed on for them to do the same, or one day we will spend our sunset years telling our children and our children's children what it was once like in the United States where men were free."[6]

We Conservatives need to get busy.

NOTES

1: On Liberty and Tyranny

1 Adam Smith, *An Inquiry into the Nature and Causes of the Wealth of Nations* (New York: Collier, 1937).

2 Russell Kirk constructed "Ten Principles of Conservatism," consisting of his own thoughts and borrowing from others. It is well worth reading. Russell Kirk, "Ten Conservative Principles" (adapted from Russell Kirk, *The Politics of Prudence* [Chicago: ISI Books, 1993]), Russell Kirk Center, http://permanentthings.com/kirk/ten-principles.html.

3 Leo Strauss, *The City and Man* (Chicago: University of Chicago Press, 1978), 6.

4 Alexis de Tocqueville, *Democracy in America* (New York: Penguin, 2003).

5 U.S. Constitution, Preamble.

6 James Madison, Alexander Hamilton, and John Jay, *The Federalist Papers* (New York: Penguin, 1987), 319–20.

7 Michael J. Gerson, *Heroic Conservatism: Why Republicans Need to Embrace America's Ideals (And Why They Deserve to Fail if They Don't* (New York: HarperCollins, 2007), 16.

8 William Kristol and David Brooks, "What Ails Conservatism," *Wall Street Journal*, Sept. 15, 1997, A22.

2: On Prudence and Progress

1 Edmund Burke, *Reflections on the Revolution in France*, ed. Frank M. Turner (New Haven, Conn.: Yale University Press, 2003), 19.

2 Peter James Stanlis, *Edmund Burke: The Enlightenment and Revolution* (Edison, N.J.: Transaction, 1991), 213, citing Edmund Burke, "A Letter to a Noble Lord," *Works*, vol. 5 (Boston: Little, Brown, 1904), 186.

3 Ibid.

4 Burke, *Reflections on the Revolution in France*, 81.

5 Mark Zaretsky, "Senator Cites Kennedy Brothers For Their Inspiration," *New Haven Register*, May 26, 2008.

6 Raymond Aron, *The Opium of the Intellectuals* (New Brunswick, N.J.: Transaction, 2007), 240–41.

7 Wilfred M. McClay, "The Idea of Change in American Politics: Meaningful Concept or Empty Promise?" Heritage Foundation, Oct. 30, 2008, http://www.heritage.org/research/thought/fp21.cfm.

8 Eric Hoffer, *The True Believer: Thoughts on the Nature of Mass Movements* (New York: Perennial, 2002), 33 (omitting footnote in original).

9 Alexander Bolton, "GOP Preps for Talk Radio Confrontation," *The Hill*, June 27, 2007, http://thehill.com/leading-the-news/gop-preps-for-talk-radio-confrontation-2007-06-27.html.

10 Senate Bill 215, "Internet Freedom Preservation Act," sponsored by Byron Dorgan, D-N.D. (to amend the Communications Act of 1934 to establish numerous "neutrality" mandates for broadband service providers). Introduced Jan. 9, 2007. http://www.gov track.us/congress/bill.xpd?bill=s110-215.

11 C. S. Lewis, *God in the Dock: Essays on Theology and Ethics*, ed. Walter Hooper (Grand Rapids, Mich.: Eerdmans, 1994), 292.

3: On Faith and the Founding

1 Anthony Flew, *There Is a God: How the World's Most Notorious Atheist Changed His Mind* (New York: HarperCollins, 2007).

2 Edmund Burke, *Selected Writings and Speeches* (Washington, D.C.: Gateway, 1997).

3 Edmund Burke, "Speech on Impeachment of Warren Hastings," May 28, 1794, http://www.notable-quotes.com/b/burke_edmund .html.

4 Alexis de Tocqueville, *Democracy in America*, 4th ed., vol. 2 (New York: Langley, 1841), 23.

5 Sharon Otterman, "Islam: Governing Under Sharia," backgrounder, Council on Foreign Relations, March 14, 2005, http:// www.cfr.org/publication/8034/#2.

6 *Everson v. Board of Ed. of Ewing*, 330 U.S. 1, 16 (1947).

7 *Everson v. Board of Ed. of Ewing*, 18.

8 Gerald T. Dunne, *Hugo Black and the Judicial Revolution* (New

York: Simon and Schuster, 1977), 269, quoting Hugo Black, Jr., *My Father* (New York: Random House, 1975), 104.

9 *Wallace v. Jaffree*, 472 U.S. 38, 107 (1985) (Rehnquist, J., dissenting).

10 Thomas G. West, "The Theology of the United States," Claremont Institute, Dec. 1, 2006, http://www.claremont.org/publica tions/pubid.30/pub_detail.asp.

11 George Washington, "Farewell Address to the People of the United States," in *The World's Famous Orations*, ed. William Jennings Bryan, vol. 8 (New York: Funk & Wagnalls, 1906), 100.

12 Barry Goldwater, "Goldwater's 1964 Acceptance Speech," Washingtonpost.com, Dec. 7, 2008, http://www.washingtonpost.com/wp-srv/politics/daily/may98/goldwaterspeech.htm.

4: On the Constitution

1 James Madison, "Letter to Henry Lee, June 25, 1824," in *The Quotable Founding Fathers: A Treasury of 2,500 Wise and Witty Quotations from the Men and Women who Created America*, ed. Buckner F. Melton, Jr. (Dulles, Va.: Brassey's, 2004), 48.

2 See, e.g., Howard Lee McBain, *The Living Constitution* (New York: Macmillan, 1927).

3 Thomas Jefferson, "Letter to Wilson Cary Nicholas, September 7, 1803," *Thomas Jefferson: Writings: Autobiography/Notes on the State of Virginia/Public and Private Papers/Addresses/Letters*, ed. Merrill D. Peterson (New York: Library of America, 1984), 1140.

4 The Ninth Amendment provides, "The enumeration in the Con-

stitution of certain rights shall not be construed to deny or disparage others retained by the people." The Tenth Amendment states: "The powers not delegated to the United States, nor prohibited by it to the States, are reserved to the States respectively, or to the people."

5 Deborah L. Rhode, "A Tribute to Justice Thurgood Marshall: Letting the Law Catch Up," *Stanford Law Review* 44 (1992), 1259.

6 Tim Wells, "A Conversation with Peter B. Edelman," *Washington Lawyer*, April 2008, http://www.dcbar.org/for_lawyers/resources/publications/washington_lawyer/april_2008/legends.cfm.

7 Stephen Breyer, *Active Liberty: Interpreting Our Democratic Constitution* (New York: Knopf, 2005).

8 Clint Bolick, *David's Hammer: The Case for an Activist Judiciary* (Washington, D.C.: Cato Institute, 2007).

9 Address of Franklin D. Roosevelt as governor of New York, March 2, 1930, http://www.lexrex.com/enlightened/writings/fdr_address.htm.

10 Ibid.

11 Franklin D. Roosevelt, "State of the Union Message to Congress, January 11, 1944," http://www.fdrlibrary.marist.edu/011144.html.

12 Ibid.

13 Ibid. (emphasis added).

14 Robin L. West, *Re-Imagining Justice: Progressive Interpretations of Formal Equality, Rights, and the Rule of Law* (Burlington, Vt.: Ashgate, 2003).

15 Ibid.

16 Bruce Ackerman, "Ackerman on Renewing the Promise of Na-

tional Citizenship," March 15, 2005, American Constitution Society for Law and Policy blog, http://www.acsblog.org/equality-and-liberty-ackerman-on-renewing-the-promise-of-national-citizenship.html.

17 U.S. Constitution, Fourteenth Amendment (emphasis added).

18 Michael W. McConnell, "Originalism and the Desegregation Decisions," *Virginia Law Review* 81 (May 1995), 947.

19 John Hinderaker, "What Liberals Want: A Progressive Conference on the Constitution Sheds Light on the Real Stakes Involved with the Judiciary," *Weekly Standard*, April 19, 2005.

20 Cass R. Sunstein, *The Second Bill of Rights: FDR's Unfinished Revolution and Why We Need It More Than Ever* (New York: Basic Books, 2004), 20–21.

21 Ralph Keyes, *The Quote Verifier: Who Said What, Where, and When* (New York: St. Martin's, 2006), 82.

22 "Interview with the Godfather: William F. Buckley, Jr., On Drugs, Universities, and the Future," *Yale Free Press*, March 2001, http://www.yale.edu/yfp/archives/01_3_buckley.html.

23 Mark R. Levin, *Men in Black: How the Supreme Court Is Destroying America* (Washington, D.C.: Regnery, 2005), 18–22.

24 Frédéric Bastiat, *The Law* (Whitefish, Mont.: Kessinger, 2004), 6.

5: On Federalism

1 Rhode Island did not send a delegation.

2 U.S. Constitution, Tenth Amendment.

3 *New State Ice Co. v. Liebmann*, 285 U.S. 262, 311 (1932) (Brandeis, J., dissenting).

4 See chapter 2, "On Prudence and Progress."

5 A lawsuit filed by Landmark Legal Foundation forced then-Oregon governor Barbara Roberts, who declared the measure "dead on arrival," to implement the voter-approved JOBS-Plus program. See *Burke v. Roberts*, Case No. 92C-11310-1 (Marion County [Oregon] Circuit Court, Sept. 23, 1993). See also Jeffrey Tryens, "Aligning Government Priorities with Societal Hopes and Expectations," testimony before U.S. House of Representatives Committee on Government Reform and Oversight, Subcommittee on Government Management, Information and Technology, Oct. 31, 1997, *Oregon's Progress Board Strategic Planning Model*, http://www.oregon.gov/DAS/OPB/jttestim.shtml. See also Howard Rolston, John K. Maniha, and Nancye Campbell, "Job Retention and Advancement in Welfare Reform," CCF Brief No. 18, Brookings Institution, March 2002, http://www.brookings.edu/papers/2002/03welfare_campbell.aspx.

6 For more than ten years Landmark Legal Foundation represented Milwaukee Parental Choice Program's author, Wisconsin state representative Annette "Polly" Williams, while successfully defending her school choice program. See *Davis v. Grover*, 480 N.W.2d 460 (Wis. 1992) and *Jackson v. Benson*, 570 N.W.2d 407 (Wis. 1998). These cases were the forerunner to the U.S. Supreme Court's decision in *Zelman v. Simmons-Harris*, 536 U.S. 639 (2002), in which Landmark also participated. See also Amanda Paulson, "Milwaukee's Lessons on School Vouchers," *Christian Science Monitor*, May 23, 2006, 1.

7 Joseph Henchman, "Momentum Builds to Repeal Maryland

Computer Services Tax," Tax Foundation, Tax Policy blog, March 14, 2008, http://www.taxfoundation.org/blog/show/23005.html; John Wagner, "Computer Services Firms Want Sales Tax Repealed," *Washington Post*, Dec. 9, 2007, C05.

8 Joseph Henchman, "MD Computer Services Tax Repealed; GA Tax Plans Die," Tax Foundation, Tax Policy blog, April 8, 2008, http://www.taxfoundation.org/blog/show/23100.html.

9 U.S. Constitution, Seventeenth Amendment.

10 U.S. Constitution, Article I, § 8, cl. 3.

11 *Wickard v. Filburn*, 317 U.S. 111 (1942).

12 Ibid.

13 U.S. Department of Labor, Bureau of Labor Statistics, "Federal Government, Excluding the Postal Service," Career Guide to Industries, March 12, 2008, http://www.bls.gov/oco/cg/cgs041.htm.

14 Lori Montgomery, "Congress Passes $3 Trillion Budget," *Washington Post*, June 6, 2008, A03.

15 16 CFR 303 et seq. (2008).

16 21 CFR 700 to 740 (2008).

17 10 CFR 430.32 (2008).

18 16 CFR 632.1 et seq. (2008).

19 "LSU Libraries Federal Agencies Directory," Louisiana State University, July 23, 2007, http://www.lib.lsu.edu/gov/fedgov.html.

20 Clyde Wayne Crews, Jr., "Ten Thousand Commandments 2007: An Annual Snapshot of the Federal Regulatory State," Competitive Enterprise Institute, 2000, 2.

21 David Keating, "A Taxing Trend: The Rise in Complexity, Forms, and Paperwork Burdens," NTU Policy Paper 124, National Taxpayers Union, April 16, 2007, 3.

22 *Prigg v. Pennsylvania*, 41 U.S. 539 (1842).

23 *Dred Scott v. Sandford*, 60 U.S. 393 (1857).

24 For a useful exposition of federalism-related arguments and the slavery question, see Ilya Somin, "Is Federalism Tainted by Slavery and Jim Crow?," Dec. 26, 2006, Volokh Conspiracy, http://volokh.com/posts/1167177535.shtml.

25 U.S. Constitution, Article I, § 9.

26 U.S. Constitution, Article I, § 2.

27 U.S. Constitution, Article IV, § 2.

28 Declaration of Independence.

29 David E. Bernstein, "Civil Rights Undermined by Antidiscrimination Laws," Foxnews.com, Feb. 4, 2004, http://www.foxnews.com/story/0,2933,110482,00.html.

30 It is worth noting that Republican support for passage of the 1964 Civil Rights Act was much stronger than Democratic support. In the House of Representatives, 80 percent (138–34) of Republicans voted for the bill as opposed to only 61 percent (152–96) of Democrats. The Senate votes in favor were 82 percent (27–6) of Republicans and 69 percent (46–11) of Democrats. See *Congressional Record*, vol. 110, June 18, 1964, 14319; *Congressional Record*, vol. 110, July 2, 1964, 15894.

31 James Madison, Alexander Hamilton, and John Jay, *The Federalist Papers* (New York: Penguin, 1987).

6: On the Free Market

1 Karl Marx, *The Communist Manifesto* (New York: Penguin, 2002).

2 Scott A. Hodge, "News to Obama: The OECD Says The United States Has The Most Progressive Tax System," Tax Foundation, Tax Policy blog, Oct. 29, 2008, http://www.taxfoundation.org/blog/show/23856.html (analysis of data presented in "Growing Unequal? Income Distribution and Poverty in OECD Countries," OECD Publishing, 2008).

3 Congressional Budget Office, "Historical Effective Federal Tax Rates: 1979–2005; Summary Table 1, Effective Tax Rates, 2004 and 2005," Dec. 2007, http://www.cbo.gov/ftpdocs/88xx/doc8885/EffectiveTaxRates.shtml#1011537.

4 Saul D. Alinsky, *Rules for Radicals* (New York: Vintage, 1971), 184.

5 Ibid., 185.

6 Peter Slevin, "For Clinton and Obama, a Common Ideological Touchstone," *Washington Post*, March 25, 2007, http://www.washingtonpost.com/wp-dyn/content/article/2007/03/24/AR2007032401152.html.

7 James Wilson, *Works of the Honourable James Wilson, L.L.D.* (Philadelphia: Lorenzo, 1804).

8 Howard Husock, "The Trillion-Dollar Shakedown that Bodes Ill for Cities," *City Journal*, Winter 2000, http://www.city-journal.org/html/10_1_the_trillion_dollar.html.

9 Stan Liebowitz, "The Real Scandal," *New York Post*, Feb. 5, 2008.

10 Ibid.

11 Ibid.

12 Howard Husock, "The Financial Crisis and the CRA," *City Journal*, Oct. 30, 2008, http://www.city-journal.org/2008/eon1030hh.html.

13 Liebowitz, "The Real Scandal."

14 Husock, "The Financial Crisis and the CRA."

15 Ibid.

16 Editorial, "Fannie Mae's Patron Saint," *Wall Street Journal*, Sept. 10, 2008; Joseph Goldstein, "Pro-Deregulation Schumer Scores Bush For Lack of Regulation," *New York Sun*, Sept. 22, 2008; Robert Novak, "Crony Image Dogs Paulson's Rescue Effort," *Chicago Sun-Times*, July 17, 2008.

17 Office of Federal Housing Enterprise Oversight, "Report of the Special Examination of Freddie Mac," Dec. 2003, http://www.ofheo.gov/media/pdf/specialreport122003.pdf; Office of Federal Housing Oversight, "Report of the Special Examination of Fannie Mae," May 2006, http://www.ofheo.gov/media/pdf/FNM SPECIALEXAM.PDF.

18 Lynnley Browning, "AIG's House of Cards," Portfolio.com, Sept. 28, 2008, http://www.portfolio.com/news-markets/top-5/2008/09/28/AIGs-Derivatives-Run-Amok.

19 Robert P. Murphy, "The Fed's Role in the Housing Bubble," Pacific Research Institute blog, http://liberty.pacificresearch.org/blog/id.271/blog_detail.asp.

20 Daniel Arnall and Alice Gomstyn, "Where Did Taxpayer Money Go? Panel Slams Treasury," ABC News, Jan. 9, 2009, http://abcnews.go.com/Business/Economy/story?id=6606296&page=1.

21 Matthew Karnitschnig, "Expanding the $700 Billion Bailout . . . to $1 Trillion," Deal Journal blog, *Wall Street Journal*, Nov. 13, 2008, http://blogs.wsj.com/deals/2008/11/13/expanding-the-700-billion-bailoutto-1-trillion/; Dan Wilchins and Johnathan Stempel, "Citigroup Gets Massive Bailout," Reuters, Nov. 24, 2008, http://www.reuters.com/article/ousiv/idUSTRE4AJ45G20081124?sp=true.

22 David Goldman, "Bailouts: $7 trillion and rising," Cnnmoney.

com, Nov. 26, 2008, http://cnnmoney.mobi/money/business/business/detail/108180/full;jsessionid=86F1E4FE7D60687998796168192A856A.

23   Barry Ritholtz. "Big Bailouts, Bigger Bucks," The Big Picture blog, Jan. 24, 2009, http://www.ritholtz.com/blog/2008/11/big-bailouts-bigger-bucks/.

24   Ibid.

25   "Economic Stimulus Package," CCH Tax Briefing, CCHgroup .com, Feb. 13, 2008, http://tax.cchgroup.com/legislation/2008-stimulus-package.pdf.

26   United States Senate Committee on Banking, Housing and Urban Affairs, "Summary of the 'Housing and Economic Recovery Act of 2008,' " June 17, 2008, http://banking.senate.gov/public/_files/HousingandEconomicRecoveryActSummary.pdf.

27   Jamie Dupree, "Just Some of the Economic Stimulus Bill," Jamie Dupree blog, Jan. 24, 2009, http://newstalkradiowhio.com/blogs/jamie_dupree/2009/01/just-some-of-the-economic-stim.html.

28   Editorial, "The Deficit Spending Blowout: The Looming Red Ink Is Unlike Anything In U.S. Peacetime History," *Wall Street Journal*, Jan. 8, 2009: A14.

29   Rahm Emanuel, "Rahm Emanuel on the Opportunities of Crisis," WSJ.com video, Nov. 19, 2008, http://online.wsj.com/video/rahm-emanuel-on-the-opportunities-of-crisis/3F6B9880-D1FD-492B-9A3D-70DBE8EB9E97.html.

30   "The Truth About Oil and Gasoline: An API Primer," American Petroleum Institute, June 6, 2008, 9, http://www.energytomorrow.org/media/resources/r_454.pdf.

31   Editorial, "Our Thorny Oil Patch," *Investor's Business Daily*, March 13, 2008, A12.

32   Max Schulz, "Energy and the Environment: Myths and Facts,"

Manhattan Institute for Policy Research, April 17, 2007, http://www.manhattan-institute.org/pdf/Energy_and_Environment_Myths.pdf.

33 "The Truth About Oil," 11.

34 Editorial, "Record Profits Mean Record Taxes," *Investor's Business Daily*, Feb. 12, 2008, A10.

35 Steven Mufson, "Ethanol Industry Gets a Boost From Bush," *Washington Post*, Jan. 25, 2007, D01.

36 Matt Crenson, "Biofuels Boom Raises Tough Questions," Associated Press, March 10, 2007.

37 Joseph A. Schumpeter, *Capitalism, Socialism, and Democracy* (New York: Harper, 1975), 82–85.

38 James Sherk, "Auto Bailout Ignores Excessive Labor Costs," Web Memo 2135, Heritage Foundation, Nov. 19, 2008, http://www.heritage.org/Research/Economy/wm2135.cfm?renderfor print=1.

39 Mickey Kaus, "Where Do Detroit's Inefficient Work Rules Come From?" Kausfiles blog, *Slate*, Dec. 9, 2008, http://www.slate.com/blogs/blogs/kausfiles/archive/2008/12/12/where-do-unproductive-work-rules-come-from.aspx.

40 Ibid.

41 Doug Bandow, "How Should America Cut Its Oil Dependency?" *Detroit News*, Nov. 30, 2007, 15A.

42 Eric Peters, "Cost Is No Object When It's For Our Own Good," online posting, Nov. 20, 2007, National Motorists Association, http://www.motorists.org/blog/cost-is-no-object-when-its-for-our-own-good/.

43 Editorial, "The Environmental Motor Company," *Wall Street Journal*, Nov. 19, 2008, A20.

44 U.S. Department of Labor, Bureau of Labor Statistics, "Union

Members Summary," Jan. 25, 2008, http://www.bls.gov/news .release/union2.nr0.htm.

45 George McGovern, "My Party Should Respect Secret Union Ballots," *Wall Street Journal*, Aug. 8, 2008, A13.

46 Will Wilkinson, "Failure: For Our Future," Fly Bottle blog, Nov. 14, 2008, http://www.willwilkinson.net/flybottle/2008/11/14/ failure-for-our-future/.

47 See Adam Smith, *An Inquiry into the Nature and Causes of the Wealth of Nations* (New York: Random House, 1994).

48 See Jim VandeHei, "Kerry Donors Include 'Benedict Arnolds,' " *Washington Post*, Feb. 26, 2004, A01.

49 Barack Obama, "The Democratic Debate in Cleveland, Feb. 26, 2008," transcript, *New York Times*, http://www.nytimes.com/ 2008/02/26/us/politics/26text-debate.html?ref=politics.

50 Jacob Funk Kirkegaard, "Offshoring, Outsourcing, and Production—Relocation—Labor Market Effects in the OECD Countries and Developing Asia," Working Paper Series, Peterson Institute for International Economics, April 2007, http://iie.com/ publications/wp/wp07-2.pdf.

51 U.S. Department of Labor, Bureau of Labor Statistics. "Labor Force Statistics from Current Population Survey, Table 1, Employment Status of the Civilian Noninstitutional Population, 1942 to Date," http://www.bls.gov/cps/cpsaatl.pdf.

52 Ibid.

53 David Levey, U.S. Department of Commerce, International Trade Administration, "2006 Was a Record for U.S. Exporters," *Invest in America*, Feb. 2007, http://www.trade.gov/press/publica tions/newsletters/ita_0207/2006_0207.asp; White House, Office of the Press Secretary, "Fact Sheet: United States and India: Stra-

tegic Partnership," March 2, 2006, http://www.whitehouse.gov/news/releases/2006/03/20060302-13.html.

54 U.S. Department of Commerce, International Trade Administration, "Impacts of FDI [Foreign Direct Investment]," *Invest in America*, http://ita.doc.gov/investamerica/impacts.asp.

55 Ibid.

56 Lawrence W. Reed, "Great Myths of the Great Depression," Mackinac Center for Public Policy, Sept. 2005, http://www.mackinac.org/archives/1998/sp1998-01.pdf.

57 Ibid.

58 Ibid.; Paul M. Johnson, *A History of the American People* (New York: HarperCollins, 1988), 740.

59 Ibid.

60 Amity Shlaes, "Don't Repeat Errors of New Deal," *New York Post*, Nov. 10, 2008.

61 Reed, "Great Myths," 15.

62 Robert VanGiezen and Albert E. Schwenk, "Compensation from before World War I through the Great Depression," U.S. Department of Labor, Bureau of Labor Statistics, Compensation and Working Conditions, Fall 2001, http://www.bls.gov/opub/cwc/cm20030124ar03p1.htm.

63 Meg Sullivan, "FDR's Policies Prolonged Depression by 7 Years, UCLA Economists Calculate," *UCLA News*, Aug. 10, 2004. See also Harold L. Cole and Lee E. Ohanian, "New Deal Policies and the Persistence of the Great Depression: A General Equilibrium Analysis," *Journal of Political Economy* 112.4 (Aug. 2004), 779–816.

64 Ibid.

65 George Allen, "Reagan Tax Cuts Lifted Americans," Townhall

.com, Aug. 13, 2007, http://townhall.com/Columnists/George Allen/2007/08/13/reagan_tax_cuts_lifted_americans.

66 Editorial, "Still Morning in America," *Wall Street Journal*, Jan. 20, 2006, A14.

67 Friedrich Hayek, *The Road to Serfdom* (Chicago: University of Chicago Press, 1994), 58.

68 Abraham Lincoln, "Reply to New York Workingmen's Democratic Republican Association, March 21, 1864," *The Collected Works of Abraham Lincoln*, ed. Roy P. Basler, vol 7 (New Brunswick, N.J.: Rutgers University Press, 1990), 259–60.

7: ON THE WELFARE STATE

1 David Walker, "Long-Term Fiscal Outlook: Action Is Needed to Avoid the Possibility of a Serious Economic Disruption in the Future," testimony before the Senate Budget Committee, General Accounting Office, Jan. 29, 2008, http://gao.gov/new.items/d08411t.pdf.

2 Ibid., 8.

3 Ibid., 17.

4 Henry Rogers Seager, *Social Insurance: A Program of Social Reform* (New York: Macmillan, 1910), 4–5.

5 Social Security Administration, "Henry Seager's 1910 Book on Social Insurance," http://www.ssa.gov/history/seager.html.

6 Geoffrey Kollmann, "Social Security: Summary of Major Changes in the Cash Benefits Program: 1935–1996," *Congressional Research Service*, Dec. 20, 1996, http://www.ssa.gov/history/pdf/crs9436.pdf.

7 Franklin D. Roosevelt, "Message to Congress Reviewing the Broad Objectives and Accomplishments of the Administration," June 8, 1934, http://www.ssa.gov/history/fdrstmts.html#message1.

8 Arthur Schlesinger, Jr., *The Coming of the New Deal* (Boston: Houghton Mifflin, 1959), 308.

9 Milton Friedman, "Social Security Socialism," *Wall Street Journal*, Jan. 26, 1999, A18.

10 Social Security Administration, "Trust Fund FAQs," June 3, 2008, http://www.ssa.gov/OACT/ProgData/fundFAQ.html.

11 Wilbur J. Cohen and Milton Friedman, *Social Security: Universal or Selective?* (Washington, D.C.: American Enterprise Institute, 1972), 36.

12 Social Security Administration, "65 Years of American Life: Social Security and Other Signs of the Times," *Oasis* 46.3 (2000), 13, http://www.ssa.gov/history/oasis/ann2000part4.pdf; Jo Anne Barnhart, testimony before the Social Security Subcommittee, House Committee on Ways and Means, May 17, 2005, http://www.ssa.gov/legislation/testimony_051705.html; Social Security Administration, "SSI Federally Administered Payments," 2004, http://www.ssa.gov/policy/docs/statcomps/ssi_monthly/2004/table01.pdf.

13 Richard Wolf, "Social Security Hits First Wave of Boomers: Drain on the System Picks up in Jan., When Millions Born in '46 Start Taking Benefits," *USA Today*, Oct. 9, 2007, 1A.

14 *Helvering v. Davis*, 301 U.S. 619, 635 (1937).

15 James Madison, "Letter to Edmund Pendleton, January 21, 1792," *The Papers of James Madison*, ed. Robert A. Rutland et al., vol. 14 (Charlottesville: University Press of Virginia, 1984).

16 Harry Truman, "Annual Message to the Congress on the State of the Union, January 7, 1948," http://www.c-span.org/executive/transcript.asp?cat=current_event&code=bush_admin&year=1948.

17 Lyndon B. Johnson, "Remarks with President Truman at the Signing in Independence of the Medicare Bill," July 30, 1965, Lyndon Baines Johnson Library and Museum, http://www.lbjlib.utexas.edu/johnson/archives.hom/speeches.hom/650730.asp.

18 Ibid.

19 Larry DeWitt, "The Medicare Program as a Capstone to the Great Society—Recent Revelations in the LBJ White House Tapes," citing White House tape WH6503.11, Lyndon Baines Johnson Library and Museum, May 2003, http://www.larrydewitt.net/Essays/MedicareDaddy.htm.

20 U.S. Department of Health and Human Services, Centers for Medicare and Medicaid Services, "Your Medicare Benefits," August 2008, http://www.medicare.gov/Publications/Pubs/pdf/10116.pdf.

21 Hoover Institution, "Facts on Policy: Medicaid and Medicare Claims," Nov. 21, 2006, http://www.hoover.org/research/factsonpolicy/facts/4680256.html.

22 Wolf, "Social Security Hits First Wave of Boomers," 1A.

23 "2007 Annual Report of The Boards of Trustees of the Federal Hospital Insurance and Federal Supplementary Medical Insurance Trust Funds," http://www.cms.hhs.gov/reportstrustfunds/downloads/tr2007.pdf.

24 Greg D'Angelo and Robert E. Moffit, "Congress Must Not Ignore the Medicare Trustees' Warning," Web Memo 1869, Heritage Foundation, March 26, 2008, 1, citing Social Security and Medi-

care Boards of Trustees, "A Message to the Public—A Summary of the 2008 Annual Reports," March 27, 2008, http://www.heritage.org/Research/Healthcare/wm1869.cfm.

25 2007 Trustees Report.

26 Hoover Institution, "Facts on Policy: Medicaid and Medicare Claims."

27 Congressional Budget Office, "The Long-Term Outlook for Health Care Spending: Appendix A—Medicare and Medicaid: An Overview," Nov. 2007, http://www.cbo.gov/ftpdocs/87xx/doc8758/AppendixA.4.1.shtml#1070033.

28 "State Expenditure Report Fiscal Year 2006," National Association of State Budget Officers, Fall 2007, 50, http://www.nasbo.org/Publications/PDFs/fy2006er.pdf.

29 Hoover Institution, "Facts on Policy: Medicare and Medicaid Claims."

30 Martha Derthick, Policymaking for Social Security (Washington, D.C.: Brookings Institution, 1979) 166.

31 Congressional Budget Office, "Long Term Economic Effects of Some Alternative Budget Policies," May 19, 2008, 8–9, http://www.cbo.gov/ftpdocs/92xx/doc9216/05-19-LongtermBudget_Letter-to-Ryan.pdf.

32 Nancy Pelosi, "Statement on 'Cover the Uninsured Week,'" press release, April 28, 2008, http://speaker.gov/30something/newsroom/pressreleases?id=0631.

33 See Carmen DeNavas-Walt, Bernadette D. Proctor, and Cheryl Hill Lee, U.S. Census Bureau, "Income, Poverty, and Health Insurance Coverage in the United States: 2005," GPO, Aug. 2006, 22 (Table 8), http://www.census.gov/prod/2006pubs/p60-231.pdf.

34 U.S. Department of Health and Human Services, "Overview of the Uninsured in the United States: An Analysis of the 2005 Current Population Survey," ASPE Issue Brief, HHS Office of the Assistant Secretary for Planning and Education, Sept. 22, 2005, 4, http://aspe.hhs.gov/health/reports/05/uninsured-cps/ib .pdf.

35 Conrad F. Meier, "Politicians Using Flawed Data of Uninsured Population," Heartland Institute, Dec. 2004, http://www.heart land.org/policybot/results.html?artId=16014.

36 Daniel Martin, "A&E Patients Left in Ambulances for up to Five Hours 'So Trusts Can Meet Government Targets,' " *Daily Mail* (London), Feb. 18, 2008.

37 Ibid.

38 Celia Hall, "Patients Wait Year for Hip Surgery," *Daily Telegraph* (London), Dec. 21, 2006.

39 Ibid.

40 Tom Leonard, "British Cancer Boy Needs £375,000 for Pioneering US Care," *Daily Telegraph* (London), Jan. 23, 2007.

41 Sarah-Kate Templeton, "NHS Dentists Play as Patients Wait," *Times of London*, March 30, 2008.

42 Sarah Lyall, "In a Dentist Shortage, British (Ouch) Do It Themselves," *New York Times*, May 7, 2006, http://www.nytimes.com/ 2006/05/07/world/europe/07teeth.html.

43 Laura Donnelly, "Don't Treat the Old and Unhealthy, Say Doctors," *Daily Telegraph* (London), Sept. 26, 2008, http://www.tele graph.co.uk/news/uknews/1576704Don't-treat-the-old-and-un healthy,-say-doctors.html.

44 Steve Brusk, "Clinton Drops Hospital Story From Stump Speech," CNN.com, April 6, 2008, http://www.cnn.com/2008/POLITICS/ 04/06/clinton.hospital/.

45 Editorial, "State Denies Cancer Treatment, Offers Suicide Instead," *WorldNetDaily*, June 19, 2008, http://www.worldnetdaily
.com/index.php?fa=PAGE.view&pageId=67565; Editorial, "Fix
This Medical Ethics Glitch," *Oregonian*, July 29, 2008.

46 Ibid.

47 Edmund Burke and Edward John Payne, *Burke, Select Works*
(Clark, N.J.: Lawbook Exchange, 2005), 71.

48 Jeffery M. Jones, "Majority of Americans Satisfied With Their
Healthcare Plans," Gallup, Nov. 29, 2007, http://www.gallup
.com/poll/102934/Majority-Americans-Satisfied-Their-Own
-Healthcare.aspx.

49 Tom Daschle, *Critical: What We Can Do About the Health-Care
Crisis* (New York: St. Martin's, 2008).

50 Tony Blankley, "Daschle-Obama Health Care Possibilities" (citing Daschle, 179), Townhall.com, Nov. 26, 2008, http://town
hall.com/columnists/TonyBlankley/2008/11/26/daschle-obama_
health_care_possibilities.

51 Blankley, "Daschle-Obama," (citing Daschle, 125).

8: ON ENVIRO-STATISM

1 George Reisman, *Capitalism: A Treatise On Economics* (Ottawa,
Ill.: Jameson, 1998), 81.

2 Gerald and Natalie Sirkin, "DDT, Fraud, and Tragedy," *American
Spectator*, Feb. 25, 2005, http://www.spectator.org/archives/2005/
02/25/ddt-fraud-and-tragedy.

3 "The Nobel Prize in Physiology or Medicine 1948," Nobel Foundation, http://nobelprize.org/nobel_prizes/medicine/laureates/
1948.

4 J. Gordon Edwards, "A Case Study in Scientific Fraud," *Journal of American Physicians and Surgeons*, 9.3 (2004).

5 Malcolm Gladwell, "The Mosquito Killer," *New Yorker*, July 2, 2001, 48.

6 Tina Rosenberg, "What the World Needs Now is DDT," *New York Times*, April 11, 2004.

7 National Academy of Sciences, *The Life Sciences*, (Washington, D.C.: National Academy of Sciences Press, 1970).

8 Rachel Carson, *Silent Spring* (Boston: Houghton Mifflin, 1962).

9 Ronald Bailey, "*Silent Spring* at 40: Rachel Carson's Classic is not Aging Well," *Reason*, June 12, 2002, www.reason.com/news/show/34823.html.

10 Rosenberg, "What the World Needs Now."

11 Gladwell, "The Mosquito Killer," 42.

12 David Brown, "WHO Urges Use of DDT in Africa," *Washington Post*, Sept. 16, 2006, A9, http://www.washingtonpost.com/wp-dyn/content/article/2006/09/15/AR2006091501012.html.

13 Marjorie Mazel Hecht, "In Africa, DDT Makes a Comeback to Save Lives," *Executive Intelligence Review*, June 18, 2004, http://www.larouchepub.com/other/2004/sci_techs/3124ddt_africa.html.

14 Steven Milloy, "Day of Reckoning for DDT Foes?" *Washington Times*, Sept. 24, 2006, http://www.washingtontimes.com/news/2006/sep/24/20060924-085112-7380r/ quoting *In the Matter of Stevens Industries, Inc., et al., L.F. & R. Docket Nos. 63, et al. (Consolidated DDT Hearings) Hearing Examiner's Recommended Findings, Conclusions, and Orders*, April 25, 1972: 93, 94.

15 Milloy, "Day of Reckoning."

16 Ibid.; Gerald and Natalie Sirkin, "Highlights of the Sierra Club's

History," Sierra Club, www.sierraclub.org/history/timeline.asp; "25 Years After DDT Ban, Bald Eagles, Osprey Numbers Soar," Environmental Defense Fund, press release, June 13, 1997, www .edf.org/pressrelease.cfm?contentID=2446.

17 Lauren Neergaad, "WHO Calls for More DDT Use vs. Malaria," CBS News, Sept. 15, 2006, http://www.cbsnews.com/stories/ 2006/09/15/ap/health/mainD8K5C8QG1.shtml.

18 Todd Seavey, "The DDT Ban Turns 30—Millions Dead of Malaria Because of Ban, More Deaths Likely," American Council on Science and Health, June 1, 2001, http://www.acsh.org/health issues/newsID.442/healthissue_detail.asp.

19 Ibid.

20 "No Compromise in Defense of Mother Earth," *Earth First! Journal*, http://www.earthfirstjournal.org/section.php?id=1&PHPSES SID=fe1e40acb1646466cd78cf4c8fc90415.

21 David M. Graber, "Mother Nature as a Hothouse Flower; The End of Nature by Bill McKibben," book review, *Los Angeles Times*, Oct. 22, 1989, 9.

22 Marc Morano, "Flush Toilets Called 'Environmental Disaster,'" Cybercast News Service, June 12, 2003, http://www.cnsnews .com/public/content/article.aspx?RsrcID=5615.

23 "Greenpeace Exhibits Bulb Innovations for the Climate at the Philips Innovation Centre," Greenpeace, press release, June 29, 2007, http://www.greenpeace.org/india/press/releases/greenpeace -exhibits-bulb-innov.

24 Helen Kennedy, "Rumsfeld Goes on the Warpath, Ready to Whip N. Korea, Too," *Daily News* (New York), Dec. 24, 2002, 3.

25 Keith Bradsher, "As Asia Keeps Cool, Scientists Worry About the Ozone Layer," *New York Times*, Feb. 23, 2007, C1.

26 Molly Millett, "Coming Clean; Green Machines—New Washers That Use Less Water and Energy—Get the Guilt Out. But They're Not Cheap," *Saint Paul Pioneer Press*, Nov. 4, 2000, E1.

27 Laura Snider, "Gas Lawn Mowers Belch Pollution, New Electric Lawn Service Comes to Boulder," *Daily Camera* (Boulder, Colo.), July 27, 2007, http://www.dailycamera.com/news/2007/jul/27/gas-lawn-mowers-belch-pollution/; Patricia Monahan, "Mow Down Pollution," *Pittsburgh Tribune-Review*, May 28, 2006, http://www.pittsburghlive.com/x/pittsburghtrib/search/s_455613.html; Matthew L. Wald, "Keep the Charcoal Off the Grill, Utilities Say," *New York Times*, May 29, 1994.

28 Editorial, "Dems' Energy Answer: Snake Oil," *Investor's Business Daily*, Nov. 27, 2006, A19.

29 Charli E. Coon, "Why the Government's CAFE Standards for Fuel Efficiency Should Be Repealed, not Increased," Backgrounder 1458, Heritage Foundation, July 11, 2001, http://www.heritage.org/Research/EnergyandEnvironment/BG1458.cfm.

30 Robert W. Crandall and John D. Graham, "The Effect of Fuel Economy Standards on Automobile Safety," 32 *Journal of Law and Economics* 97 (Jan. 1989), 118.

31 Julie DeFalco, "The Deadly Effects of Fuel Economy Standards: CAFE's Lethal Impact on Auto Safety," Competitive Enterprise Institute, June 1999, http://cei.org/PDFs/cafe2.pdf.

32 James R. Healey, "Death by the Gallon," *USA Today*, July 2, 1999, B1.

33 Paul R. Portney et al., *Effectiveness and Impact of Corporate Average Fuel Economy (CAFE) Standards* (Washington, D.C.: National Academy, 2002), 3. See also Paul R. Portney et al., "Statement before U.S. Senate Committee on Commerce, Sci-

ence, and Transportation and Committee on Energy and Natural Resources Aug. 2, 2001," http://www7.nationalacademies.org/ocga/testimony/Fuel_Economy_Standards.asp.

34 John Adams, *The Works of John Adams, Second President of the United States: With a Life of the Author, Notes and Illustrations*, vol. 6 (Boston: Little, Brown, 1851), 9.

35 Ronald D. Utt, "Will Sprawl Gobble Up America's Land? Federal Data Reveal Development's Trivial Impact," Backgrounder 1556, Heritage Foundation, March 30, 2002, http://www.heritage.org/Research/SmartGrowth/BG1556.cfm.

36 Ibid.

37 Victor Cohen, "U.S. Scientist Sees New Ice Age Coming," *Washington Post*, July 9, 1971, A4.

38 "Another Ice Age," *Time*, June 24, 1974. (Professor Reid, who is considered the father of modern climatology, publicly repudiated his "global cooling" predictions and went on to become a leader among scientists critical of man-made global warming fearmongering. See Steven H. Schneider, "Against Instant Books," *Nature*, Dec. 22/29, 1977, 650.)

39 Peter Gwynne, "The Cooling World," *Newsweek*, April 28, 1975.

40 Sharon Begley, "Global Warming Is a Cause of This Year's Extreme Weather," *Newsweek*, July 7, 2008, http://www.newsweek.com/id/143787/output.

41 Richard Lindzen, "Global Warming Debate Is More Politics Than Science, According to Climate Expert," *Environment & Climate News* (Heartland Institute), Nov. 1, 2004, http://www.heartland.org/Article.cfm?artId=15893.

42 Alex Massie and Toby Harnden, "World 'At Tipping Point

Over Global Warming," *Daily Telegraph* (London), Feb. 17, 2007, 15.

43 Phil McKenna, "Al Gore Rallies US Congress Over Climate," *New Scientist*, March 22, 2007, http://environment.newscientist .com/channel/earth/dn11437.

44 Scott Shepard, "A Push for 'Green Conservatism'; Gingrich, Like Kerry, Backs Global Warming Action," *Atlanta Journal-Constitution*, April 11, 2007, A9.

45 Ibid.

46 David Roach, "Gore Cites Political Will, Claims Scriptural Mandate on Environmental Issues," *Baptist Press*, Jan. 31, 2008, http://www.bpnews.net/printerfriendly.asp?ID=27293.

47 Transcript, *Today* show, NBC News, Nov. 5, 2007.

48 Brian Montopoli, "Scott Pelley and Catherine Herrick on Global Warming Coverage," Public Eye blog, March 23, 2006, CBSNews .com, http://www.cbsnews.com/blogs/2006/03/22/publiceye/entry 1431768.shtml.

49 Robert James Bidinotto, "Environmentalism: Freedom for the 90s," *Freeman Ideas on Liberty*, Nov. 11, 1990.

50 Ronald Bailey, "Who is Maurice Strong?" *National Review*, Sept. 1, 1997.

51 Michael E. Mann, Raymond S. Bradley, and Malcolm K. Hughes, "Northern Hemisphere Temperatures During the Past Millennium: Inferences, Uncertainties, and Limitations," *Geophysical Research Letters* 26 (1999), 759–62.

52 Thomas Hayden, "Science: Fighting Over a Hockey Stick," *U.S. News & World Report*, July 14, 2005, http://www.usnews.com/usnews/culture/articles/050714/14climate.htm; "Climate Change 2001: The Scientific Basis," esp. chapter 2, Intergovernmental

Panel on Climate Change, http://www.ipcc.ch/ipccreports/tar/
wg1/pdf/TAR-02.PDF.

53 Edward J. Wegman, David W. Scott, and Yasmin H. Said, "Ad
Hoc Committee Report on the Hockey Stick Global Climate
Reconstruction," July 11, 2006, http://www.climateaudit.org/pdf/
others/07142006_Wegman_Report.pdf.

54 Edward J. Wegman, testimony before the House Committee on
Energy and Commerce, July 27, 2006, 3, http://www.urban-
renaissance.org/urbanren/publications/Wegman%5B1%5D.pdf.

55 Lubos Motl, "Vaclav Klaus on Global Warming," Reference
Frame blog, Feb. 10, 2007, (translation of interview in *Harspdar-
ske Noviny*, Feb. 8, 2007), http://epw.senate.gov/public/index
.cfm?FuseAction=Minority.Blogs&ContentRecord_id=B6CD77
13-802A-23AD-4AAF-A2D2ADDB287F.

56 James M. Taylor, "IPCC Author Selection Process Plagued by
Bias, Cronyism: Study," *Environment & Climate News*, Heartland
Institute, Sept. 2008.

57 Ibid.

58 "Climate Change 2007: Synthesis Report, Summary for Policy-
makers," Intergovernmental Panel on Climate Change, Nov.
12/17, 2007.

59 Ibid.

60 S. Fred Singer and Dennis T. Avery, *Unstoppable Global Warming:
Every 1,500 Years* (New York: Rowman & Littlefield, 2007).

61 Tim Ball and Tom Harris, "New Findings Indicate Today's Greenhouse Gas Levels Not Unusual," *Canada Free Press*, May 14, 2007,
http://www.canadafreepress.com/2007/global-warming051407
.htm.

62 Lawrence Solomon, "Limited role for CO_2, The Deniers—Part

X," *National Post* (Canada), Nov. 28, 2006, http://www.national post.com/story.html?id=069cb5b2-7d81-4a8e-825d-56e0f112aeb 5&k=0.

63 Dudley J. Hughes, "Carbon Dioxide Levels Are a Blessing, Not a Problem," *Environment & Climate News*, Heartland Institute, May 1, 2007, http://www.heartland.org/policybot/results.html? articleid=20952.

64 National Oceanic and Atmospheric Administration, "Greenhouse Gases Frequently Asked Questions," Dec. 1, 2005, http:// lwf.ncdc.noaa.gov/oa/climate/gases.html; "The *Real* Inconvenient Truth," Junkscience.com, Aug. 2007, http://www.junk science.com/Greenhouse/.

65 Casey Lartigue and Ryan Balis, "The Lieberman-Warner Cap and Trade Bill: Quick Summary and Analysis," National Policy Analysis No. 570, National Center for Public Policy Research, June 2008, http://www.nationalcenter.org/NPA570.html.

66 See "Earth's 'Fever' Breaks: Global COOLING Currently Under Way," Inhofe EPW Press blog, Feb. 27, 2008, U.S. Senate Committee on Environment and Public Works, http://epw.senate.gov/ public/index.cfm?FuseAction=Minority.Blogs&ContentRecord_ id=5CEAEDB7-802A-23AD-4BFE-9E32747616F9.

67 Phil Chapman, "Sorry to Ruin The Fun, But an Ice Age Cometh," *Australian*, April 23, 2008, 14.

68 James Hansen, "Global Warming Twenty Years Later: Tipping Points Near," June 24, 2008, http://www.columbia.edu/~jeh1/ 2008/TwentyYearsLater_20080623.pdf.

69 Christopher Booker, "The World Has Never Seen Such a Freezing Act," Telegraph.co.uk, Nov. 16, 2008, http://www.telegraph .co.uk/opinion/main.jhtml?xml=/opinion/2008/11/16/do1610 .xml.

70 William W. Beach et al., "The Economic Costs of the Lieberman-Warner Climate Change Legislation," Heritage Center for Data Analysis Report No. 08-02, Heritage Foundation, May 12, 2008.

71 David Derbyshire, "Every Adult in Britain Should Be Forced to Carry 'Carbon Ration Cards,' Say MPs," *Daily Mail* (London), May 27, 2008.

72 California Energy Commission, "2008 Building Energy Efficiency Standards for Residential and Nonresidential Buildings," Commission Proposed Standards Nov. 2007, http://www.energy.ca .gov/2007publications/CEC-400-2007-017/CEC-400-2007-017 -45DAY.PDF.

73 U.S. Environmental Protection Agency, "Regulating Greenhouse Gas Emissions Under the Clean Air Act," Advanced Notice of Rulemaking July 30, 2008, http://www.epa.gov/fedrgstr/EPA -AIR/2008/July/Day-30/a16432a.pdf.

74 John Brignell, "A Complete List of Things Caused by Global Warming," *Numberwatch*, July 16, 2008, http://www.number watch.co.uk/warmlist.htm; "Over 500 Things Caused by Global Warming," Church of Global Warming, http://churchofglobal warming.com/index.php?option=com_content&task=view&id= 50&Itemid=1.

75 Jonathan H. Adler, "Stand or Deliver: Citizen Suits, Standing, and Environmental Protection," *Duke Environmental Law and Policy Forum* 12 (Fall 2001) 39, 42.

76 Sierra Club Awards, Sierra Club, http://www.sierraclub.org/ awards/descriptions.

77 *Massachusetts v. EPA*, 549 U.S. 497 (2007).

78 Mark P. Mills, "Brownout," *Forbes*, June 5, 2008, http://www .forbes.com/forbes/2008/0630/038.html.

79 Ibid.

80 Ibid.

81 Keith Johnson, "Steven Chu: 'Coal Is My Worst Nightmare,'" online posting, December 11, 2008; Environmental Capital blog, *Wall Street Journal*, Feb. 2, 2009, http://blogs.wsj.com/environ mentalcapital/2008/12/11/steven-chu-coal-is-my-worst-nightmare/.

82 Steven Dinan, "Obama Climate Czar Has Socialist Ties," *Washington Times*, January 12, 2009, http://www.washingtontimes.com/ news/2009/jan/12/obama-climate-czar-has-socialist-ties/; Agenda, "XXIII Congress of the Socialist International, Athens Global Solidarity: The *Courage* to Make a *Difference*," June 30, 2002–July 2, 2002 (listing Carol Browner as panel speaker and "Member of Socialist International Commission for a Sustainable World Society"), http://www.socialistinternational.org/viewArticle.cfm? ArticlePageID=1272.

83 Thomas Friedman, *The Colbert Report*, transcript, *Comedy Central*, Nov. 20, 2008.

9: On Immigration

1 Edward J. Erler, Thomas G. West, and John Marini, *The Founders on Citizenship and Immigration: Principles and Challenges in America* (Lanham, Md.: Rowman & Littlefield, 2007).

2 Otis Graham, "A Vast Social Experiment," forum paper, *Negative Population Growth*, 2005, http://www.npg.org/forum_series/social exp.html.

3 William McGowan, "The 1965 Immigration Reforms and the *New York Times*: Context, Coverage, and Long-Term Consequences," Center for Immigration Studies, August 2008 (citing

Graham; *Congressional Digest*, May 1965, p. 152), http://www.cis
.org/articles/2008/back908.pdf.

4 Graham (quoting William Miller, *New York Times*, Sept. 8, 1964,
p. 14).

5 "Three Decades of Mass Immigration," Center for Immigration
Studies, Sept. 1995, http://www.cis.org/articles/1995/back395
.html.

6 Ibid.

7 Steven Malanga, "How Unskilled Immigrants Hurt Our Economy," *City Journal*, Summer 2006, http://www.city-journal.org/
html/16_3_immigrants_economy.html.

8 Edwin Meese, "An Amnesty by Any Other Name . . ." commen-
tary, Heritage Foundation, May 25, 2006, http://www.heritage
.org/press/commentary/ed052406a.cfm.

9 Theodore H. White, *America in Search of Itself: The Making of the
President 1956–1980* (New York: Warner, 1982).

10 David G. Gutierrez, *Walls and Mirrors: Mexican Americans, Mexican Immigrants, and the Politics of Ethnicity* (Berkeley: University
of California Press, 1995).

11 Steve Sailer, "Cesar Chavez, Minuteman," *American Conserva-.
tive*, Feb. 27, 2006.

12 Samuel Lubell, *The Future of American Politics*, 3rd ed. (New York:
Harper Colophon, 1965).

13 See "2004 National Election Pool Exit Polls," CNN.com, http://
www.cnn.com/ELECTION/2004/pages/results/states/US/P/00/
epolls.0.html; "2008 National Election Pool Exit Polls," CNN
.com, http://www.cnn.com/ELECTION/2008/results/polls/#USP
00p1.

14 U.S. Constitution, Fourteenth Amendment (emphasis added).

15 Steven A. Camarota, "Immigrants in the United States, 2007,"
    Backgrounder 1007, Center for Immigration Studies, Nov. 2007,
    http://www.cis.org/articles/2007/back1007.pdf.

16 Jeffrey S. Passel, "Estimates of the Size and Characteristics of the
    Undocumented Population," Pew Hispanic Center, March 21,
    2005, http://pewhispanic.org/files/reports/44.pdf.

17 U.S. Census Bureau, "Facts for Features, Hispanic Heritage
    Month 2008: Sept. 15–Oct. 15," Sept. 8, 2008, http://www
    .census.gov/Press-Release/www/releases/archives/cb08ff-15.pdf.

18 Robert J. Samuelson, "Importing Poverty," *Washington Post*, Sept.
    5, 2007, A21.

19 Ibid.

20 Heather Mac Donald, "Hispanic Family Values?" *City Journal*,
    Autumn 2006, http://www.city-journal.org/html/16_4_hispanic_
    family_values.html.

21 Camarota, "Immigrants."

22 Richard Fry and Felisa Gonzales, "One-in-Five and Growing Fast:
    A Profile of Hispanic Public School Students," Pew Hispanic
    Center, Aug. 26, 2008, http://pewhispanic.org/files/reports/92
    .pdf.

23 U.S. Census Bureau, "2007 American Community Survey: Se-
    lected Social Characteristics in the United States: 2005–2007,"
    http://factfinder.census.gov/servlet/ADPTable?_bm=y&-geo_
    id=01000US&-qr_name=ACS_2007_3YR_G00_DP3YR2&-ds
    _name=ACS_2007_3YR_G00_&-_lang=en&-_sse=on.

24 Robert J. Samuelson, "Build a Fence—And Amnesty," *Washing-
    ton Post*, March 8, 2006, A19.

25 Robert Rector, "Amnesty and Continued Low-Skill Immigration
    Will Substantially Raise Welfare Costs and Poverty," Back-

grounder 1936, Heritage Foundation, May 16, 2006, http://www .heritage.org/Research/Immigration/bg1936.cfm.

26 Jacob L. Vigdor, "Measuring Immigrant Assimilation in the United States," *Manhattan Institute Civic Report*, May 2008, http:// www.manhattan-institute.org/pdf/cr_53.pdf.

27 George Washington, "Farewell Address to the People of the United States," *The World's Famous Orations*, ed. William Jennings Bryan, vol. 8 (New York: Funk & Wagnalls, 1906), 90.

28 Samuel P. Huntington, "The Hispanic Challenge," *Foreign Policy*, March–April 2004.

29 St. Augustine, *City of God* (New York: Penguin, 1984).

30 Alexis de Tocqueville, *Democracy in America* (New York: Penguin, 2003).

31 John Perazzo, "Hillary's Open Borders Disgrace," FrontPageMag azine.com, April 24, 2007, http://www.frontpagemag.com/Arti cles/Read.aspx?GUID=473b1006-dea4-4340-b1a2-ac0838de 5714.

32 Ibid.

33 Interview with Juan Hernandez, *Nightline*, ABC News, June 7, 2001.

34 Thomas Sowell, "Border Scheme Built On Fraud, Empty Promises," *Baltimore Sun*, June 14, 2007, 23A.

35 Mark Krikorian, "Jobs Americans Won't Do," *National Review Online*, Jan. 7, 2004, http://www.nationalreview.com/comment/ krikorian200401070923.asp.

36 Steve Hanke, "Mexico Mimics Yugoslavia," *National Post's Financial Post & FP Investing* (Canada) Apr. 21, 2006, FP19.

37 George J. Borjas, "Increasing the Supply of Labor Through Immigration, Measuring the Impact on Native-born Workers,"

Center for Immigration Studies, May 2004, http://www.cis.org/articles/2004/back504.pdf.

38 Lee Cary, "When Illegal Immigration Trends Converge," *American Thinker*, Feb. 24, 2008, http://www.americanthinker.com/2008/02/when_illegal_immigration_trend.html.

39 Peter Brimelow, "Milton Friedman at 85," *Forbes*, Dec. 29, 1997, 52.

40 Louis Uchitelle, "Plan May Lure More to Enter U.S. Illegally, Experts Say," *New York Times*, Jan. 9, 2004, A12.

41 Robert Rector and Christine Kim, "The Fiscal Costs of Low-Skill Immigrants to the U.S. Taxpayer," Special Report 14, Heritage Foundation, May 21, 2007, http://www.heritage.org/Research/Immigration/upload/sr_14.pdf.

42 Cary, "When Illegal Immigration Trends Converge," quoting Eugene McCarthy, *A Colony of the World: The United States Today: America's Senior Statesman Warns His Countrymen* (New York: Hippocrene, 1992), 71.

43 U.S. Department of Justice, "National Youth Gang Survey 1999–2001," Office of Justice Programs, Office of Juvenile Justice and Delinquency Prevention, National Youth Gang Center, July 2006, http://www.ncjrs.gov/pdffiles1/ojjdp/209392.pdf.

44 Chris Swecker (FBI Criminal Investigative Division), testimony before the Subcommittee on the Western Hemisphere, House International Relations Committee, April 20, 2005, http://www.fbi.gov/congress/congress05/swecker042005.htm.

45 Government Accountability Office, "Information on Criminal Aliens Incarcerated in Federal and State Prisons and Local Jails," April 7, 2005, 2–3, http://www.gao.gov/new.items/d05337r.pdf.

46 Ibid., 1.

47 Madeleine Pelner Cosman, "Illegal Aliens and American Medicine," *Journal of American Physicians and Surgeons* 10.1 (Spring 2005), 6, http://www.jpands.org/vol10no1/cosman.pdf.

48 Ibid.

49 Ibid.

50 William Harms, "Lomnitz: Understanding History of Corruption in Mexico," *University of Chicago Chronicle* 15.6, Nov. 27, 1995, http://chronicle.uchicago.edu/951127/lomnitz.shtml.

51 The quotation in Spanish reads: "He afirmado con orgullo que la Nación Mexicana se extiende más allá de sus fronteras y que los migrantes mexicanos son una parte importante de ella." Ernesto Zedillo, "Mensaje del presidente de México, Dr. Ernesto Zedillo Ponce de León, en la cena ofrecida con motivo de la Conferencia Anual del Consejo Nacional de la Raza," website of the president of the Mexican Republic, July 23, 1997, http://zedillo.presiden cia.gob.mx/pages/disc/jul97/23jul97-2.html.

52 "Results of poll of U.S., Mexican citizens," United Press International, June 12, 2002.

53 Heather Mac Donald, "Mexico's Undiplomatic Diplomats," *City Journal*, Fall 2005, 28–41, http://www.city-journal.org/html/15_4_ mexico.html.

54 Ibid.

55 Ibid.

56 Ibid.

57 Rene Romo, "Kemp Touts Self-Sufficiency in N.M.," *Albuquerque Journal*, Oct. 25, 1996, A1.

58 Alexander Hamilton, *The Works of Alexander Hamilton*, vol. 8 (New York: Putnam, 1904), 289.

59 Ibid.

60 Robert Rector, "Senate Immigration Bill Would Allow 100 Million New Legal Immigrants over the Next Twenty Years," Web Memo 1076, Heritage Foundation, May 15, 2006, www.heritage.org/research/immigration/wm1076.cfm.

10: On Self-Preservation

1 James Madison, Alexander Hamilton, and John Jay, *The Federalist Papers*, ed. Isaac Kramick (New York: Penguin, 1987), 98–99.

2 U.S. Constitution, Article I, Section 8.

3 See S. E. Forman, *A Brief History of the American People* (New York: Century, 1922), 155–56; Adrienne Koch, *Jefferson & Madison—The Great Collaboration* (New York: Knopf, 1950), 141–42; George Washington, "Farewell Address to the People of the United States," *The World's Famous Orations*, ed. William Jennings Bryan, vol. 8 (New York: Funk & Wagnalls, 1906).

4 Washington, "Farewell Address," 94.

5 George Washington, "First Annual Message to Congress," Jan. 8, 1790, http://avalon.law.yale.edu/18th_century/washs01.asp.

6 George Washington, "Fifth Annual Message to Congress," Dec. 3, 1793, http://avalon.law.yale.edu/18th_century/washs05.asp.

7 Thomas G. West, "The Progressive Movement and the Transformation of American Politics," online posting, Heritage Foundation, July 18, 2007, http://www.heritage.org/research/though/fp12.cfm.

8 Colleen A. Sheehan, *Friends of the Constitution: Writings of the "Other" Federalists, 1787–1788*, ed. Colleen A. Sheehan and Gary L. McDowell (Indianapolis: Liberty Fund, 1998). Online

edition posting James Wilson speech to the Pennsylvania State House, Oct. 6, 1787, *Online Library of Liberty*, http://oll.liberty fund.org/title/2069/156165.

9 George Will interview with William F. Buckley, Jr., *This Week with George Stephanopoulos*, transcript, ABC News, Oct. 9, 2005, http://abcnews.go.com/ThisWeek/TheList/story?id=119 7559.

10 George Will, "A War Still Seeking a Mission," *Washington Post*, Sept. 11, 2007, A17.

11 Barack Obama, "The American Moment: Remarks to the Chicago Council on Global Affairs," BarackObama.com, April 23, 2007, http://www.barackobama.com/2007/04/23/the_american_moment_remarks_to.php.

12 Barack Obama, "Speech, Berlin, Germany," transcript, ABC News, July 24, 2008, http://abcnews.go.com/Politics/Vote2008/story?id=5442292&page=.

13 Patrick Goodenough, "U.S. Expected to Reverse Course on United Nations," CNSNews.com, Nov. 7, 2008, http://www.cnsnews.com/public/content/article.aspx?RsrcID=38988.

14 Michael T. Klare, "Obama's Energy Challenge," TheNation.com, Nov. 10, 2008, http://www.thenation.com/doc/20081124/klare.

15 Editorial, "Would Democrats Waterboard Atta?" *Investor's Business Daily*, Dec. 12, 2007, http://www.ibdeditorials.com/IBDArticles.aspx?id=282355009929237.

16 See Mark R. Levin, "The Outrage of *Hamdan*," And Another Thing blog, June 29, 2006, *National Review* Online, http://levin.nationalreview.com/post/?q=ZDY0NThhMDc5OGYzOWM3M zFhYTQxNTYzNzEyZDJiYjQ.

17 Andrew C. McCarthy, "The Patriot Act Under Siege," online
    posting, Nov. 13, 2003, *National Review* Online, Dec. 8, 2008,
    http://www.nationalreview.com/comment/mccarthy2003111308
    35.asp.

18 *Korematsu v. United States*, 323 U.S. 214 (1944).

19 Jen Christensen, "FBI tracked King's every move," CNN.com,
    April 7, 2008, http://www.cnn.com/2008/US/03/31/mlk.fbi.con
    spiracy/index.html.

20 "Echelon; Worldwide Conversations Being Received By The
    Echelon System May Fall Into The Wrong Hands And Innocent
    People May Be Tagged As Spies," transcript, *60 Minutes*, Feb. 27,
    2000, *Cryptome*, March 2, 2000, http://cryptome.info/echelon
    -60min.htm.

Epilogue: A Conservative Manifesto

1 Candy Crowley interview with George W. Bush, "Bush on Economy, Iraq, Legacy," CNN, Dec. 16, 2008, http://www.cnn.com/
   video/#/video/politics/2008/12/16/intv.crowley.bush.long.cnn?
   iref=videosearch.

2 Avalon Project, available at http://avalon.law.yale.edu/.

3 Atlas Economic Research Foundation available at http://www
   .atlasusa.org/V2/main/page.php?page_id=385.

4 National Archives and Records Administration, Ronald Reagan,
   "Remarks at a Conservative Political Action Conference Dinner," February 26, 1982, Public Papers of Ronald Reagan, Ronald
   Reagan Presidential Library, http://www.reagan.utexas.edu/
   archives/speeches/1982/22682b.htm.

5 See Milton and Rose Friedman, *Free to Choose: A Personal State-ment* (New York: Harcourt, 1980), Appendix B.

6 Ronald Reagan, "Encroaching Control (The Peril of Ever Expanding Government)," *A Time for Choosing: The Speeches of Ronald Reagan 1961–1982*, ed. Alfred A. Baltizer and Gerald M. Bonetto (Chicago: Regnery, 1983), 38.